A BO... ...ATION
OF SPIRITUAL LEADERS

SUFFERING
While
SERVING

DR. MARK T. GIBSON

SUFFERING *While* SERVING

Copyright @ 2024 Dr. Mark T. Gibson
ISBN: 9798876844842
All rights reserved.

Author owns complete rights to this book and may be contracted in regards to distribution. Printed in the United States of America.

Library of Congress Cataloging-in-Publication Data

The copyright laws of the United States of America protect this book. No part of this publication may be reproduced or stored in a retrieval system for commercial gain or profit.

No part of this publication may be stored electronically or otherwise transmitted in any form or by any means (electronic, photocopy, recording) without written permission of the author except as provided by USA copyright law.

The Holy Bible, King James Version (KJV) . Amplified (AMP) Copyright © 1954, 1958, 1962, 1964, 1965, 1987 by The Lockman Foundation

shero publishing

Editing: SynergyEd Consulting/ synergyedconsulting.com
Graphics & Cover Design: Greenlight Creations Graphics Designs
glightcreations.com/ glightcreations@gmail.com

Be it advised that all information within this literary work, *Suffering While Serving* has been acknowledged to be the truthful accounts of each co-author. The co-authors are responsible for their contributions and chapter accuracy and hold SHERO Publishing harmless for any legal action arising as a result of their participation in this publication.

SUFFERING *While* SERVING

Table of Contents

Dedication			5
Preface			6

~Co-Author Chapters~

Chapter 1	Reverend Tracy Bell	A Thorn In My Flesh	10
Chapter 2	Reverend A. D. Black	Crossed Over: Tragedy to Triumph	22
Chapter 3	Pastor Jamal H. Brown	Servant: Love Thyself	36
Chapter 4	Dr. Mark T. Gibson	Bleeding While Leading	50
Chapter 5	Minister Janice Hawkins	Wounded	64
Chapter 6	Elder LaFonza Koger	I Had To Go Through Something	76
Chapter 7	Reverend Terry D. Lee	Grieving is a Process	90
Chapter 8	Reverend Alphonso Lewis	The Walking Wounded	104
Chapter 9	Dr. Gregory K. Moss	A Triple Storm	124
Chapter 10	Pastor Johnnie Randolph, Jr	I Waited	140
Chapter 11	Reverend Lillie Sanders	Suffering on Purpose for A Purpose	154
Chapter 12	Dr. Shawn J. Singleton	Suffering in Silence	168
Chapter 13	Reverend Dr. Joe L. Stevenson	Loving and Serving God in the Off Season	182
Chapter 14	Pastor Frank T. White, Sr.	Triumphantly Traversing the Trauma	196
Chapter 15	Elder Bonita Womack	God's Grace is Sufficient	210
Chapter 16	Dr. James T. Worthy	Physician, Heal Thyself?	224

Dedication

This book of spiritual leaders is dedicated to every leader suffering in silence. We pray that our stories will drive you to realize that you are not alone, and support is waiting to lift and encourage you. To every leader, let's lock arms to encourage each other and remove the cycle of **Suffering While Serving** others.

Preface

Reverend Dr. Martin Luther King, Jr. said, "Everybody can be great because everybody can serve", simplistic and yet so profound. His life exemplified the pure essence of not self, but others. Dr. King displayed the call for all to give of ourselves, through service for the greater good of humanity in the face of racism, hatred, and division in our society. The death threats, physical and verbal abuse, incarcerations, demoralizing acts inflicted upon him, and ultimately his assassination became the example of what it means to "suffering while serving."

There is an illusion that ascending to a role of leadership is full of great accolades, popularity, glitz, and glamour. Everyone will cooperate with your personality and leadership style, your vision will be accepted and adhered to, you will be celebrated for the hard decisions that must be made. This notion is as far from the truth, whether you are called to lead a Fortune 500 company, a church as a pastor, or an auxiliary within a church or community. There's an adage which holds true to this day, "Heavy is the head that wears the Crown." Many leaders spend more time working long after the employees have retired for the day or even the week, because of the ultimate responsibility that will rest upon him/her. Leaders will be celebrated and criticized in the same moment, and they must be willing to endure pain, misunderstandings, expectations, and demands of the role for which they hold. Their own desires and conveniences now become secondary to the great cause, and there are times when this sacrifice will cause the leader to suffer while still providing service to those who are looking to them.

The collection of journeys, of which you are about to embark, are actual stories from a collection of pastors, ministers, and ministry leaders. Their boldness in being transparent about their suffering while leading in the church is designed to help those who are suffering in silence. While this project is designed for others to identify with the stories, it is our ultimate prayer that the suffering leader/reader will seek the necessary help to work through any issues that seem to hold one captive. The pressures and expectations of leaders can become overwhelming, and it affects one's mental and spiritual stability. Suffering while serving is a reality for many of our leaders within the faith community, particularly with the office of the pastor. These stories are not solely for the pastor, but for the parishioner to understand that the serving in leadership is not relegated to Sunday mornings…it is a seven day per week and twenty-four hour per day sacrifice that is made for the greater cause and body. Pastors and leaders, once they accept their calls, never "clock out" from the work that they have committed themselves.

It is easy for leaders to mask their pain and suffering to not draw attention to their shortcomings of severe emotional and spiritual pain that they are enduring. The recognition of their pain while still holding up the banner of hope is what plagues our pulpits, pews and effective promises, and there is a need to identify those who are willing to intentionally interrupt our internal isolation. Too many leaders are paralyzed by the pains of their pasts and working through their present paralysis will always penalize the promises of who they can and should become.

A BOOK COMPILATION FROM SPIRITUAL LEADERS

SUFFERING *While* SERVING

Chapter 1

Rev. Tracy Bell

Rev. Tracy Bell

Tracy J. Bell was born in Raleigh, North Carolina in April of 1962. He was raised in Garner and was a graduate of Garner Senior High School class of 1980. Following graduation, Tracy studied Business Administration at Wake Technical Community College before his enlistment into the United States Navy, where he served faithfully. After serving his country in the United States Navy, Tracy was employed by the North Carolina Department of Corrections, where he also served faithfully for many years before stepping out on faith to become an entrepreneur in the cleaning industry, where he founded B&J Carpet and Upholstery Cleaning.

In time, Pastor Tracy developed an unquenchable love and thirst for people to meet Jesus in the early 90s following his own personal "Road to Damascus" encounter. Tracy Bell knew that his mission was to reflect the life and love of Jesus Christ wherever he went. He has carried this message for nearly 30 years to those who were living in alleys, homeless shelters, Hurricane Katrina victims, and even to the devasted rocky roads of Haiti. On each journey, Tracy saw the same thing; people with value, a purpose, and a destiny to fulfill. Pastor Tracy Bell was ordained as a deacon at Poplar Springs Christian Church in 1995 and served faithfully until his calling into the ministry to preach and teach the gospel. Tracy was installed as the assistant pastor of Poplar Springs Christian Church in the early 2000s. Pastor Bell and his lovely wife Mary both completed their master's degrees in ministry at Justice Fellowship College International in 2008. In 2013, Pastor Tracy J. Bell was installed as the Senior Pastor of New Bethel Christian Church in Raleigh, North Carolina with his amazing wife, Mary, and their four wonderful children by his side. Pastor Tracy recently wrote his first book entitled, *The Remarkable You*, which was written to enlighten the reader that all of us have something remarkable in us that is waiting to be discovered. One of his favorite scriptures continues to be Psalm 8:1- *Oh Lord our Lord, How Excellent is Your name in all the earth!!!*

"A Thorn in My Flesh"

And lest I should be exalted above measure by the abundance of the revelations, a thorn in the flesh was given to me, a messenger of Satan to buffet me, lest I be exalted above measure. Concerning this thing I pleaded with the Lord three times that it might depart from me. And He said to me, "My grace is sufficient for you, for My strength is made perfect in weakness." Therefore, most gladly I will rather boast in my infirmities, that the power of Christ may rest upon me. Therefore, I take pleasure in infirmities, in reproaches, in needs, in persecutions, in distresses, for Christ's sake. For when I am weak, then I am strong.
2nd Corinthians 12:7-10

Though Paul reminds me and a multitude of others who find ourselves between a rock and a hard place to stand confidently on God's Word, thorns are painful, uncomfortable, and downright hurt to the core. Regardless of what it looks like, feels like, or sounds like, the pastors that I know, crave God's comfort, peace, and provisions to accompany us, as we wholeheartedly attempt to make true disciples out of ordinary people. Though Paul reminds us in the scriptures that God may use satanic, thorny messengers to humble us so that He can build us, this process is not only uncomfortable but often dark and sometimes depressing.

I commend Paul for reaching a place in His life where he was able to boast and embrace his personal infirmities, reproaches, persecutions, and distresses so that the power of God would rest upon him. However, I must honestly admit that I am not there yet, and only God knows the exact number of straws it will take before my back breaks. I am still at a place in ministry where I long for God to move every thorn, demonic mindset, and unnecessary weight out of my way. Though many of us are aware that the Lord uses fiery trials to build our patience, our character, and our faith, I submit that many of us would have chosen another route, if we knew the sufferings that awaited us in pastoring.

I equally submit that it has been the darkness that has caused my light to shine. It has been the heavy loads and thorny trials that have brought strength, maturity, and a richer walk with God into my life. I would have never known the faithfulness of God without experiencing the wiles of the devil. God allowed Satan to hinder and humble me so that He could reveal to me how desperately I needed Him daily. Just as Joseph's very own brothers attempted to do him harm instead of good, God has also conditioned my heart to render nothing but His goodness whenever whoever does whatever behind my back.

I have had a ringside seat to observe the masterful tricks that Satan uses to keep the children of God in bondage by directing their focus to their will being done on earth instead of God's Will. Unknowingly, many saints have clung to their will tighter than the Will of God. Therefore, I have chosen to have compassion for them instead of vengeance. On another note, many saints have become comfortably stuck in traditions and the way they were taught regardless of the liberty that is at hand to walk as Kingdom people. As a senior pastor, I have seen multiple self-centered individuals solicit my time and energy to build on their foundation instead of the one that Jesus Christ has called me to build upon. It is these such entities that have caused me to understand why God needs true shepherds that will follow His voice even when others cease to follow pastors that He has sent to lead them safely home.

As I meditate on the thorn in the flesh that Apostle Paul dealt with, I am reminded of my times as a child when we would pick wild blackberries in the woods or alongside the roadside in rural areas. Picking wild blackberries was one way of having a delicious treat while hiking through the woods. If we picked enough, mom would end up baking one of her wonderful cobblers or a blackberry pie for dinner.

There was one small, but painful issue with selecting these ripe blackberries. They had thorns all around them! As plump, ripe, and sweet as they may have been, there was also a cost in retrieving these berries. Though we didn't have to pay a dime for these berries, they often cost us a little bit of our blood thanks to the thorns. At the end of the day, I looked forward to a melt-in-your-mouth fresh baked cobbler. However, the thorns in my flesh, scratches on my hand, and sometimes the blooddrops that followed the piercing of the thorns, reminded me that there was a cost for every serving I ate. No matter how carefully I attempted to select from the thorny vine, the thorns managed to stick me.

This is what the ministry has done to me over the years. God has never stuck me, but Satan has managed to figure out how to stick me in the midst of my attempt to bring glory to God. Though I believe in giving people opportunities to grow, mature, and thrive, the thorns of Satan also had a way of looming near the berry only to hinder me. Having said that, I would add that the devil has not been my biggest issue, but his influence on those that you would think knew better. Satan has a way of causing true believers to view their perspective because of how they see it. Satan has a way of causing believers to be blinded from truth, based on their feelings or traditions. True believers have often chosen to side with family and friends instead of the Word of God and may find a scripture to justify their actions.

As I look closer at the deception of Satan, I am reminded that these deceptive practices can be traced back to Adam and Eve in the Garden. Satan masterminded an ordeal that cost mankind what had been freely given. Out of the abundance of trees they could partake of, Satan suggested another perception that catered to mankind's flesh, and the invitation was accepted.

This deception continues to work today. Though I strive as a pastor to thrive by reaching the lost and building up the weak, I still often get stuck, pierced, and stabbed in multiple ways at multiple times in ministry. Time is what tells on all of us. Unfortunately, it is only a matter of time before the true nature of a person and their intentions are revealed. It is at these times that a shepherd is left with the task of corralling sheep lest they also go astray. Many sheep may be in the building on Sunday morning, but their hearts and minds stray. They may be active in the ministry and show up regularly, but their focus often strays onto the suggestions that Satan presents in their hearts and minds.

Satan's goal is to divide and conquer. Satan understands the strength of the people of God when their focus is on Kingdom-building! Therefore, just as he attempted to distract and discourage Nehemiah from doing a great work on the wall, Nehemiah and those who worked beside him stayed focused on the vision instead of the voices of the enemy. Nehemiah had every reason to be distracted, disgusted, discouraged, and a depressed leader, but he never stopped building.

Personally, I've often found myself in a state of being distracted, disgusted, discouraged, and a depressed leader. When COVID-19 came to town, I found myself in a state of focusing more on COVID-19, at times, rather than building. Nevertheless, by the Grace of God, I managed to stay on the wall and preach and teach the Word of God. Though many strayed away due to the alarming health reports, a few leaders and I managed to stay on the wall and build. Once the COVID scare was lifted, many still chose to stay away but went everywhere else. Perhaps their hearts were never in God's hands, and COVID was used as their way of escape. This was like another thorn that left me feeling disgusted, discouraged, distracted and a bit depressed, probably because I was expected to stay on the wall as a pastor and build regardless. So, I did! There has always been a greater expectation for me to fulfill my position over others fulfilling their position. Perhaps this mentality is based on a salary, but as I recall, Nehemiah did not build the wall all by himself. Nehemiah was able to complete the given task because his leadership had a mind to work. All that were on the wall had a mind to work!

Breaches In the Wall

It can be extremely challenging as a pastor who loves God, to look to your left and your right and see breaches in the wall, which may give access to the enemy. Breaches in a wall means that there are breaks, holes, cracks, and gaps in the wall, which gives the enemy access. Spiritually speaking, these breaches give Satan access to thwart Kingdom-building. We know that "No Weapon That Forms Against Us Shall Prosper", yet these holes, cracks, and gaps can delay what God has sent. As I recall during Daniel's time of prayer and fasting, God sent exactly what Daniel needed right away. However, the Word was delayed, causing the archangel Michael to come to the rescue.

I have often seen the work that I believe God has called me to do, be delayed because of breaches, cracks, holes, and gaps in hearts that should be fortified with sound doctrine. Again, as a pastor, I have found myself feeling some kind of way due to masterful tricks and delusions that the enemy dangles like a carrot on the perspective, perception, and feelings of the people of God. At the end of the day, I find that I have been stuck again, pierced again, and vulnerably penetrated while working on the wall.

I could go on for days about the times of stress that stem from the breaches of hearts that allow the enemy to delay. These breaches have often pulled me from family time, vacation time, personal time, and even time with God to patch up what principalities in high places have penetrated. Though I know that it is the enemy at work behind the scenes to stress and discourage, it has been very difficult to relay this to certain sheep, because they know what they know, and they feel what they feel.

The Conclusion of The Matter

Earlier Paul said that he took pleasure in his infirmities, reproaches, needs, persecutions, and distresses, for Christ's sake, because his weakness receives strength from God. I have not yet found it too pleasuring to be stuck, poked, or stabbed by the thorns of pastoring. Though I've been enlightened in scripture that pain has a purpose, the process is still lengthy. Though I know that my Abba Father would never put more on me than I can bear, infirmities are still painful, reproaches still discourage me, and persecution is still difficult.

I submit to you that I believe that the only reason that I am not on the medications that I could be on is solely due to the fact of abiding in The Secret Place of the Most-High God. I submit that I do not have any dependency on any substances or people due to the fact that I often make my way under the shadow of The Most-High. I get headaches sometimes and ponder on situations late at night at times. Yet I know that there is a God who is able to do exceedingly and abundantly more in a second than I can do in 30 years of pastoring. Though I have never seen the face of Jesus or seen the wings of an angel, I am still persuaded that nothing shall ever be able to separate me from the Love of God. Though I still fight fear with my faith and fight wrong with His Word, my heart continually says, "Yes!" I can still say, "Yes", because I can see glimpses of victory every now and then. I can still say, "Yes", because I am reminded that Job said, "Yes" when he was at his lowest in life. I still say, "Yes" because Jesus said, "Yes" to a crown of thorns. Though He was innocent, Jesus laid down His life for a multitude of people, like me, who were antichrist before He stepped in. Likewise, I have learned to forgive people who likely won't even ask for forgiveness. Most will be too prideful to ever ask, yet I've released them because the weight is much too heavy for me to carry. I've also forgiven those in the community who vowed to support, but for whatever reason took a different route. The Joy of the Lord is still my strength.

If any pastor or ministry leader who is reading this is in need of a prayer partner, please seek God for one. Until then you're more than welcome to reach out to me. Though the road appears long, the night looks dark, and the load is heavy, please believe me when I say, there is a God that is more than able. There is a God that will not let you down. The same God that came through for Moses, Job, David, and Abraham is going to come through for those of us who have relentlessly placed our faith in His hands. Be encouraged and remember that THIS TOO SHALL PAST!!

Chapter 2

Reverend A.D. Black

Rev A.D. Black

Rev. Black is a native of Washington, DC. He is an Associate Minister at Galilee Baptist Church under the leadership of Rev. Dr. Lloyd T. McGriff. As a member of Galilee, Rev. Black has been active in several ministries conducting seminars on finance and housing and speaking at the Men's Conference. He also taught at the Discipleship Institute of Galilee, about developing a personal relationship with God and discipleship. He also serves as a member of the Galilee Community Development Corporation Board of Directors.

Rev. Black is the writer and facilitator of several seminars: "Men and Their Broken Relationships", "God's Women and the Power of Persuasion" and "From Tragedy to Triumph," a seminar about losing a loved one. He is the writer of the forthcoming play, "Never Knew Love Like This Before", which is based on the book of "Hosea", and the author of the forth coming book, "Into Your Hands I Commit My Spirit," a book about taking a leap of faith.

Rev. Black is the creator and owner of CrossedOver.org, a new, exciting, interactive social media platform changing the way we share information; the founder and owner of Bac2Eden gospel radio show; a Christian motivational speaker, and gospel comedian. Rev. Black retired from the Washington Metropolitan Area Transit Authority after 42 years of service.

Rev. Black is married to the former Benita Davis of Arlington, Virginia. They have three children. Antrévyn, Ashyur'di and AJor'n.

"You are one thought from a blessing: one decision from a breakthrough".

Trust in the Lord with all your heart and lean not to your own understanding. In all your ways, acknowledge him, and he will make your paths straight.
Proverbs 3: 5-6

Crossed Over: From Tragedy to Triumph

ANY GIVEN SUNDAY

It started like any other Sunday morning. I was getting ready to lead worship at church. Normally, I watch Channel 4 news as I get dressed, but I don't remember watching that morning. After church, my family and I went shopping. Around noon, my oldest son's mom called to speak with me. I said, "What is it? I'll talk to Tré." She said "No, Anthony, I really need to speak with you."

She was so persistent that I assumed Tré had either been called back to duty or he had gotten some young lady pregnant. I thought he may have been called back to duty because after serving two terms in Iraq, he was given special permission to be stationed at Ft. Belvoir. Secondly, I had talked to Tré about getting someone pregnant. I told him that if he got someone pregnant and he's not married to her, he must tell me and must tell me the wedding date. I had told him, "You're not going to repeat that cycle; that's definitely out. That's unacceptable. You won't do what your daddy did. You'll be a much better man than I was." You don't want another man raising your child, even if he's a good man. You want to step up to the plate. I mean, how much influence would you have if you only get to be with your child from Friday to Sunday evening?

I started calling Tré's cell phone repeatedly-he doesn't answer. His mom calls me again and I tell her I'm trying to reach Tré and I'll call her back." I call his sister –she hadn't talked to Tré. Tré's mom and I agreed to meet at Tysons Corner that evening. That's when she told me about the shooting and that Tré didn't make it.

The young man that was with Tré was shot eight times and survived. Tré was shot once—he didn't survive. As Tré's mom told me what had happened, she hugged me; later, my wife told me that I didn't hug her back. I guess I was in shock. I just couldn't believe what she was saying to me; it didn't make sense.

Now, get this, a lot my friends saw the news and knew about the shooting, but not one of them called to tell me that I'd lost my son. I'm the only one in the dark. I truly believe God only wanted Tré's mom to tell me this tragic news.

At that time, I was in my late 30's early 40's, and I'd never experienced the death of a loved one in my life. As crazy as it sounds, I thought I was going leave here without experiencing it. No one close to me had ever gone from *Labor to Reward*. No way would I have thought it would be one of my children!

I called my family members, but it still didn't register that my child is gone. As a minister, I console other people. I know the protocol and what you do. So, I'm in that mode because, in my mind, it really hasn't happened to my child. When I look at it, I see the hands of God working behind the scenes on this particular Sunday—the Sunday that changed my life.

GOD WORKING BEHIND THE SCENES

I'll tell you, the time between finding out you've lost a loved one and the burial is excruciating. So many things run through your mind. I tried to recall the last time that I spoke with and saw Tré. I thought of all the things I wished I'd done and should have done.

Tré always called me during the week. I remember the last time we talked was on Father's Day the week before he passed. He's always call me late in the afternoon on Father's Day and I'd tease him saying, "Oh, I don't matter. You just call me after you call everybody else." But, that particular Father's Day, he called me early. He said, "This early enough?" I thanked him and we laughed. I tried to get the last message from his phone and save it so that I could always hear his voice.

The last time I saw Tré, we met at the car dealership where was having his new Mazda 6 repaired. As we left dealership, he stuck his hand out the window and waved, "bye daddy." My God, what I wouldn't do to get that back. I had no idea he really meant, *"Bye Daddy."*

We had to deal with detectives and things of that nature because Tré's death was a homicide. So much was going through my mind, but my main focus was my child. The pain was excruciating to say the least. Again, it's my first time dealing with a loved one's death and I don't know what I'm doing. I'm completely out of my mind, but I'm trying to hold it together because I have a wife and two other children. I'm praying and talking to God, trying to figure out how this happened. But, I still had things to do. I'm still *Minister Black*.

The biggest regret I have is not going to church the following Sunday. A terrible, terrible mistake. Why not go to the place where people can love on you? Why not go to God's house where you can get help? God knows I hadn't had to deal with this before, but now, I would be at the church before doors opened.

My church, Galilee Baptist Church, put on a beautiful homegoing service. I thank God for them and for allowing us to have the service there. The military showed up and showed out. My job, Metro (WMATA) brought a busload of people to the service. But I was really in a fog; it was like a dream.

After service, people came and asked how I was doing, but that was just a surface "how are you doing?" Of course, I'm Minister Black, I know God, I'm supposed to be okay. But nobody pulled me aside and said, "Black, how are you **really**, doing?" I've come to believe that people really don't want to know the depths of that pain, especially when it's a child and they have children. Please be clear, they're not happy that it happened to you, but they're sure glad it didn't happen to them.

What I'm trying to say is they would prefer it didn't happen at all.

My job sent me to get counseling. At my first session, I told my counselor, "I'm Minister Black. I'm a child of the Lord. I know my son is with the Lord." Second session, the same; third session, I began the speech, and my counselor says, "Whoa, Mr. Black. You've told me about the Lord, how much you love the Lord, how much He loves you, how great Heaven is, and that you know your son is there. Well, if you know your son is there and it's such a great a place, is there a greater place for your son to be?" Now, she wasn't a Christian counselor, and that struck me. Yes, you're right! My son is with God and all of us want to get to the Lord and Savior Jesus Christ. There isn't a better place that Tré could be. Am I sad and disappointed that he's gone so soon? Yes! But he is with the Lord. I got myself together and got back to doing the things that I did for church. I needed this counselor. She's now a lifelong friend.

I tell you; one phone call can change your life forever. The loss of a loved one, if you don't already know, teaches you to take life one day at a time.

Tré called me after being sworn into the Army. I wanted to be sure he'd be with the Lord, so we went over Romans 10:9 again. Tré said he believed God, but he had some questions. I laughed and said we all do. Then, Tré said, "daddy they're calling me." I wanted to ask who, but I was afraid of the answer. I had given Tré a Bible with his name engraved and the book, "Man In The Mirror." I told him that God would bring him home if he modeled his life after these two. A strange thing happened when Tré returned home. I kept hearing this little voice saying, "you really should be praying now." I didn't understand why I should be praying so hard then. After all, Tré was safely home. I understand it NOW!

THE QUESTION EVERY CHILD OF GOD MUST ANSWER IN THE STORM (Though He Slay Me, Yet Will I Trust Him)

I don't remember much about the Summer of 2005, except that I spent most of it in my basement in a fetal position crying and talking to God. The only time that I left my house was to go to church.

I know the Christian community condemns suicide and I understand. Most people think suicidal people want to hurt themselves. Although it may be true in some cases, I believe they just want the pain to stop. Would you consider the use of alcohol or drugs to cope with life's painful experiences suicide?

I'm talking about that pain when you cry out with your mouth open and nothing comes out, but you hear dogs barking in the alley 'cause only they can hear that frequency. That pain where everything about you aches. Unless you've experienced that kind of pain maybe you can't understand what I'm saying.

I remember what I call those Job days where he says to God "blot out the day I was born..." (Job 3:3). Yes, God and I would go through it in my Job sessions. I would say, *"God, you promised that you would take care of my kids; you promised that you would take care of my family, if I preached for you. I've done my part and you haven't held up your part. I'm never going to preach again so just leave me alone."* And, like He did with Job, God said, *"Anthony, you are right. I could have done it another way; I could have done somebody else's child. It's a million ways I could have done this, but I did it to Tré. Now, I have something to ask you, Anthony. Do you still love me and do you still trust me?"*

I believe every Christian must answer this profound question if you're going to walk with the Lord through the storms, when life has torn you down, when you know that the God we serve could have excused you from this pain, and you know God could have changed the outcome but, instead, He allowed you to be in the storm. Do you still love Him and do you still trust Him? Will you still love Him? Will you still trust Him through the storm? I'll tell you, everything about me said no, but my soul said yes! In the worst situation and in the worst parts of my life, never have I experienced this kind of pain. Yet, I still love You, God and I still trust You; I will love You and I will trust You!

SUMMER MADNESS

June 2006, what I call Summer Madness. I'd become so scared of the summer and here's why. June 2005, Tré was shot; June 2006, I spend the summer at the homicide trial; June 2007, my wife and other son are in a terrible car accident.

I'm at work when I get a call that my wife and son were being medevacked to separate hospitals. A nurse lets me speak to my son. I tell him "Daddy will be there. Daddy is on his way!" My son responds, "Okay, Daddy". But I don't get to speak to my wife. I rushed to Washington Hospital Center where the physician tells me pretty much that my wife is dead; they're trying to keep her comfortable until I can get the family there. My wife has glass in her eyes and hair, cuts on her face and she's unconscious. Remember, this is two years after my son was taken from me. As I'm coming out of the ER, the nurse tells me I can call whomever I needed to call. Instinctively, I turned to her, and said "No, no, no, who I need to call is already here. You guys just do your job. My Lord and Savior Jesus is already here."

I then go to Children's hospital, and I see my son playing. He says, "Hey Daddy." His nurse pulls me aside and said, "Your son is a remarkable young man to see his mother being Medevacked in another helicopter. He didn't cry; he didn't do anything. The fact that he knew you were on your way really calmed him down." I thanked her and assured my son that his mom was okay.

My son and I slept for 30 days on wooden chairs in my wife's hospital room while she was in a coma. Thank God, she survived! I knew that if I lost my wife and son, God would comfort me somehow. I'm not going to tell you that I wouldn't have been half crazy for a while, but I knew God would comfort me and get me through. He had sustained and carried me through the lowest point of my life.

It's Summer 2007. I hadn't been to work for two Summers straight. I dreaded Memorial Day weekend because, in mind, something terrible was going to happen—it had every summer since 2005. But, like they say, each storm prepares you for the next. Having lost my son, I knew the comfort, caring, and love of the Lord. So, I wasn't in panic mode.

I got through the summer. Then comes Labor Day weekend, and guess what? I get sick. I don't return to work until January. For two years I was terrified of something happening in my life during the summer. But that's how life is sometimes. Your mind can play tricks on you and you'll become scared of things that haven't happened yet.

OK GOD, NOW WHAT?
The Birthing of CrossedOver.org
(From Tragedy to Triumph)

Now what, God? What is my purpose? I'm just stumbling through life after my son's death. Then, I had to eulogize my cousin.

While talking about the expense of putting my cousin's obituary in the newspaper, God gave me the vision for CrossedOver.com. What am I supposed to do with this, God? What's the benefit? I tell you if it's ordained by God, He'll give you what you need. God gave me everything I needed from the color schemes, contents, people, and resources. I used my own money; no borrowing or investors. What started as a FREE website to memorialize loved ones who've gone from Labor to Reward now celebrates all life events. We've also partnered with organizations to serve the needs of our community. It'll sustain itself—it's free. Go to CrossedOver.org

Out of the pain of losing my son, Sgt. AnTrévyn Mason-Black, God gave me a way to keep him alive through the birth of CrossedOver.com. I don't believe CrossedOver.com would've been birthed had I lost my mother or my wife. I don't think I'd have had the strength or push to do it for anyone other than my children. I could have dealt with my mother's death, what's it called-the law of attrition-she's older; she'll go before me. My wife: would have stung me, that's my life partner. But my child! I'm not supposed to bury my child; my child is supposed to bury me.

I truly believe that out of life's pain we're supposed to birth something beautiful—*your* **Tragedy** *will birth a* **Triumph**!

Chapter 3

Elder Jamal H. Brown

Elder Jamal H. Brown

Reverend Jamal H. Brown, MDiv was born and raised by his parents, Joseph and Beverly Brown of Bronx, New York. He was raised in a village of people affectionately known as the Parklane Crew.

He moved to Elizabeth City to attend Elizabeth City State University and completed his bachelor's degree in criminal justice from Elizabeth City State University in 1993. He received his master's in divinity with a concentration in Clinical Pastoral Counseling from Shaw University in 2011. He also completed and received certification in Family Wellness Life Skills Coaching. Reverend Brown is the proud Pastor and Servant Leader of Holly Springs United Church of Christ for which he and his wife, Lady Shandolyn Brown (RN) have served since 2013.

Under their leadership, Holly Springs has seen growth and served the community in various capacities beyond the church walls. Service has expanded through a world pandemic; the adversity actually provided new opportunities. Together the church congregation has celebrated a 150-year church anniversary and the experience of God's provision to pay the church debt off during the pandemic.

Pastor Brown has been business entrepreneur since 2011 and utilizes this skill set to work with families, small business owners, clergy, and churches in the areas of final expense benefits, wealth preservation, asset accumulation, and legacy creation. What this means is that he seeks to be an effective and genuine financial resource by helping the clients he serves understand, evaluate, and implement proven strategies. The real benefit is his strategic process helps the clients he serves to minimize taxation and maximize their dollars while meeting in a more favorable setting.

Pastor Brown believes the call of the church is to be God's vehicle through the sharing and experiencing of God's gospel of Jesus Christ in the building of God's community of believers. He envisions fostering unity among believers where the love of Christ is a shared experience for all believers. Pastor Brown is a proponent of community involvement for the individual believer and the church. Over the years, Pastor Brown and Holly Springs United Church of Christ have partnered with Lost Sheep Ministry (Pastor Phil Brickle) and Woodhaven Baptist Church (Pastor Dave Stratton), on the Compassion Day event. It is a movement of bringing local churches of different faiths together in common love, respect, and understanding to help the community.

Pastor Brown is also a proud member of the Southern Conference of the United Church of Christ. He has served on several boards, including the Church and Ministry Board of Directors, and The Historic Franklinton Center of Bricks Board of Directors. In addition, he has represented the church body of Holly Springs at several annual meetings, such as the General Annual Synod of the United Church of Christ.

He is currently working on his first published book project which is a collaborative work that shall be released in the latter part of 2023. He is very excited and proud of this work. He believes that God has equipped each of us with various gifts to serve our immediate community and worldwide community to achieve spiritual, emotional, physical, and economic empowerment.

On a personal level, Pastor Brown loves traveling and spending time with his family. Pastor Brown states that his greatest accomplishment in life other than his relationship with Christ has been being happily married to Shandolyn since 1997. She is an accomplished Registered Nurse, having graduated from North Carolina Central University, and is in her field of practice, offering physical and emotional healing to her patients in the Triangle Area. They have four children: Immanuel who is serving in the US Navy, Alexcia, a teacher and actress, Candace, a financial representative in a local bank, and Charitee, a graduate of Campbell University, with a degree in Wealth and Trust Management. Pastor Brown and his wife also helped to raise Daquan Render, their niece, Daesha Adair, and Ricardo Thorpe into responsible adulthood.

To connect with Pastor Brown:
Facebook: Jamal Brown
Email: jhb4christ@yahoo.com
trinityinsurancegroup7@gmail.com

Servant: Love Thyself

This chapter mission is to inspire and motivate the servants of God and humanity to the purpose of self-care and love for oneself. My desire is to inspire the servant leaders of God by providing the reasons why we should love ourselves. It is my goal to help reshape some cultural norms to help us heal and serve God and humanity in more effective and efficient ways. We will explore ways to minimize burnout and decrease suicide among clergy. The chapter will also facilitate a greater understanding of how to foster healthier relationships between the cleric, stronger relationships with God whom we are called to serve, and better relationships with our families and the communities we are commissioned to love and guide.

The focal verse of this manuscript comes from, Matthew 22:36-39 "Teacher, which commandment in the law is the greatest?" Jesus answered him, "Love the Lord your God with every passion of your heart, with all the energy of your being, and with every thought that is within you.' This is the great and supreme commandment. And the second is like it in importance: 'You must love your friend in the same way you love yourself.' Contained within these commandments to love you will find all the meaning of the Law and the Prophets."

This scripture when studied, informs us that all that Christ suffered for us was in turn with the purpose in mind to have the supreme love ethic of loving God, loving oneself, and properly loving our neighbor and friends.

However, I believe we have missed the mark in God's mission statement of the cross; with Christ in his suffering and crucifixion. I believe the purpose of Christ's suffering was to restore us back to a healthy relationship with God, then ourselves, and then our neighbors.

We are certainly called to serve, and scripture certainly calls us to have a servant's heart as a leader. Jesus declared,

"Whoever is going to be greatest among us, let them serve". And it is written- "For even the Son of Man did not come to be served, but to serve, and to give his life as a ransom for many." Mark 10: 45 NIV

However, in our desire to serve the Lord properly, we may have missed the mark of the true posture and purpose of the Master's suffering. It is my belief now, that the intention of the Master's suffering was to be redemptive; to be an example of a keyword which is "RELATIONSHIP". We are called to be in *relationship* and the one relationship that I have seen and witnessed amongst clergy which still needs the redemptive power of God applied, is with ourselves regarding self-love. I'm not talking about a self-absorbed, narcissistic kind of love; but a healthy kind of love that allows and fosters a healthy relationship first with ourselves, and in turn cultivates a healthy relationship with God and others.

Let's explore the issue as I see it. We are called to serve others, yet we've faltered in our personal relationship with ourselves; many times, at the detriment of our personal health, families, and marriages. We have not often taught our congregants how to love us properly and in a healthy way. As a result, the weight of the ministry has caused an epidemic number of pastors to falter under the weight of the superhuman expectations of the service to others.

According to statistics from *The Urban Ministry*, that impact pastors and their families;
- 70% of pastors continually battle depression.
- 80% of pastor wives feel pressured to be someone they are not and do things they are not called to do in the church.
- 80% of pastors and 85% of their spouses feel discouraged in their roles.
- 70% feel isolated and do not have a close friend, confidant, or mentor.
- Over 50% of pastors' wives feel that their husbands' entering ministry was the worst thing to ever happen to their families.
- The severe obesity of many clergy, particularly African American male pastors, contributes to many dying prematurely, or suffering from major health problems like hypertension, diabetes, heart issues, anxiety, and depression.

These statistics are staggering, and this is just a select few to show the impact on the health of the clergy. I no longer believe this is what God called Christ to suffer for and I believe this trend and the expectations are not in alignment with the scriptural commandment to love our neighbor as we love ourselves. However, all is not lost and I believe God is never without a witness and following Christ will bring us to a fulfilled and healthy life through having meaningful and healthy relationships.

I believe if we really look at the scriptural text and the mandate on *love*. We can't really love God or our neighbor properly until we first love ourselves. I believe it's healthy to love on you first and appreciate the value and gift God has placed in each of us, without the fear of intimidation and marginalization.

Author Marianne Williamson in her poem, "Our Deepest Fear" quotes, "You are a child of God. You're playing small does not serve the world. There's nothing enlightened about shrinking so that other people won't feel insecure around you. We were born to make manifest the glory of God that is within us."

Scripture teaches that we are created in God's image and likeness, that we are fearfully and wonderfully made. So, therefore, we as clergy count, and God expects us to value our health and life. They are gifts that should be appreciated and valued. This appreciation should first come from us regarding setting healthy boundaries, seeking areas of self-awareness, and promoting personal growth and development. God's voice in the focal verse should not just impact us personally regarding love but is also communal and is created to inform and guide us regarding tradition and culture. In the same text, God tells us, and this can be found in the Old Testament and the New Testament, *contained within these commandments to love you will find all the meaning of the Law and the Prophets.* When we look at this from this proper lens God says this love commandment is what gives meaning and interpretation to the law (principles) and prophets (traditions and culture). Matthew 22:40 TPT

Therefore, we are mandated to love ourselves as part of God's will for humanity, but we can't love ourselves until we value and like us the way God does. So, we need to see ourselves through the prism of God's eyes and heart.

Relevant Question: How do I love myself and serve and love my GOD and neighbor properly?

Mental Health and Therapy

My suggestions come from observation and personal experience. To help my cohorts in the ministry achieve the needed balance of loving themselves as part of God's requirement to live life fully and do ministry effectively, I offer the following suggestions. I was raised in a church tradition that often frowned against getting therapy as a pastor and even as a Christian. So, I often rejected the notion of seeing a therapist. I believed that all I needed to do was pray and like many of my predecessors just power through the walls that were closing in on me. This caused me to have anxiety episodes and I've struggled with my weight. While pastoring, during this time, I was going through a crisis with the church and taking care of my ailing mother as her primary care giver. This all occurred and culminated while pastoring the church through a worldwide pandemic.

Many times, I would feel alone, abandoned, misunderstood, and betrayed. Believe it or not, there were thoughts of quitting and sometimes feeling like my family, friends, and church would be better off if I just wasn't here. As I was in this wilderness of confusion and self-discovery, I would often talk to my mother and wife about some of my feelings. During this time, my mother would always keep saying, "Jamal this season is for you, and God is trying to give you something." She would always encourage me and say, "Life is going to hit all of us, but we have to make a decision to *keep living* and grow, or we can shrivel up and die." Growth is truly about transformation and elevation. This can only occur when we a willing to let go of the old and grasp hold of the new.

During this time, my mom and I had a debate on an issue, and I stated to her, "Momma, that's not how you raised me". She responded and said something that was so profound to me, and it began my journey of transformation. She said in her motherly voice as only Beverly Brown could say, "Jamal, I have a right to change my position." It was as if she was giving me permission to readjust my life by changing my thinking. It was during this time that I had a chance meeting with my big brother in the ministry, Pastor Bell, at a restaurant. During our conversation, he mentioned a therapy group. As a result, that introduced me to Dr. Alphonso Lewis. I believe this was Jesus extending his hands to save me from drowning in the sea of confusion, chaos, and conflict. I was, as my therapist would say, a train wreck ready to happen and my family was going to suffer the aftermath of my derailment. I remember vividly, in what I believe was my first or second therapy session with Dr Lewis, where I was pouring out my heart, and he was tentatively listening. I mentioned something about my wife and my children, and he said something that stopped me cold in the framework of my thinking. He said to me, "Jamal, what good is it going to be if you're putting all this energy out there, helping everyone else, saving everyone else, and you have a life crisis, you have a heart attack, you have a stroke or even die?" He paused to allow me to reflect and then he continued, "Jamal, who's immediately left in the aftermath? I was at home at the time, and my therapist asked if my wife was available and if I would ask her to come into the room. Once she joined us, Dr. Lewis began to ask her some questions, and I'll never forget this as long as I live. As he asked her the questions, tears began to run down my wife's face, and I saw her concern and her pain. Her pain was real, and it came from watching me struggle to stay afloat. How I was living my life was breaking her. It was at that moment that I realized the error of my thinking and the error of my behavior regarding the impact of not loving myself properly.

It was through these therapy sessions that I have learned the importance of loving myself as part of my own ministry. I've learned the importance of prioritizing my own self-care as an important part of ministry.

However, the most powerful thing I'm discovering through therapy is- I'm discovering Jamal. One of the blessings of my therapy sessions is becoming self-aware and I was diagnosed with Adult Attention Deficit. I say this is a blessing because I'm discovering how to train myself to be better and put systems and people in place to help me be healthy and efficient in my personal life, work, and ministry in the church. One of the areas in which I'm improving is how to be actively present when I'm on dates with my wife or I'm spending time with my children. I haven't mastered it yet, but I've improved and I'm a continued work in progress.

I'm more than just a pastor, husband, father, friend, colleague, and to some, even an adversary. I'm learning to love and respect Jamal, the human being. I've got good traits and some areas that still need improvement. Through therapy, I'm understanding why God who is holy, can love a man like David, and still say he is a man after his own heart. I wish I could go deeper into this chapter regarding my therapy sessions and what I've learned but I want to encourage my fellow pastors and laborers to think of counseling and therapy as an opportunity to allow yourself to be ministered to and healed.

Relational Expectations

As a result of rediscovering myself and learning to love me, I've been empowered to understand and implement relational boundaries and expectations. I've found that in loving yourself and learning to understand your true value, you inevitably teach others how to love and respect you. It's important to know that we are human, and therefore as pastors, we cannot allow the plethora of hats we wear and obligations we shoulder, to overshadow our first ministry to ourselves, and then to our own marriages and children. We must learn to utilize the boundary of "No" with wisdom. We cannot be all things to all people, that's God's job. He himself is the only great "I AM" and we must direct our congregations to Him.

In loving ourselves, we must also always seek to make our relationship with God very personal so that He can fill us regularly and not just during times preparing a sermon. I'm suggesting times set aside for intimacy with God so He can show each of us ourselves and most importantly, Himself in revelatory ways. I'm in a season right now as I'm writing this chapter where God is showing me the right thing is not always the God thing. I'm perplexed, to be honest, but I'm enjoying what is being revealed.

Life Board of Directors and Mentors

My final observation is one of accountability and support systems. The scripture teaches that in the multitude of counsel, there is safety. I believe it is within this spirit of being whole and loving to ourselves that we can effectively minister to God's people out of a cup that is consistently being filled. We should always have mentors or individuals that we respect and who can speak the truth to us from a genuine place of wanting us to grow and be the best version of ourselves. Every business or successful organization has a board of directors and mentors to aid their organizations to operate effectively and efficiently. I believe it's important to have individuals in my life who can hold me accountable to develop into the best version of myself in each area of my life. I have couples that inspire and support me and my wife in our marriage. I have a coach who helps me with my health. I have a therapist; I have business mentors and a host of clergy mentors. My point is to encourage my brothers and sisters in the ministry to ask God for guidance and provision of people you can trust, who will allow you to be vulnerable and yet hold you accountable without being judgmental, so that we can grow and be all that God has called us to be. This will allow us to lead from a place of wholeness instead of a place of emptiness and exhaustion.

Chapter 4

Dr. Mark T. Gibson
Book Visionary

Dr. Mark T. Gibson

Rev. Dr. Mark T. Gibson is the Senior Pastor of Redeeming Love Missionary Baptist Church of Raleigh, NC. A native of Washington, DC, he holds a Bachelor's degree in Political Science from Johnson C. Smith University in Charlotte, NC, a Master's degree in Student Personnel Services from Indiana University of Pennsylvania, a Master's of Divinity from Shaw University's School of Divinity, and an earned Doctorate in Ministry from Campbell University's Divinity School. He retired from higher education as a Student Affairs professional after 32 years of service. Pastor Mark is the Co-Founder and CEO of Black Gospel Classics Radio, an internet station for Gospel Music lovers of Classic Gospel Music. He is the morning host of "The Gospel According to Mark" Monday – Friday from 7am – 10am. (www.blackgospelclassics.com)

Dr. Gibson remains passionate about serving the community through his work with various community organizations. He works with the Raleigh Interdenominational Ministerial Alliance; mentors to area elementary schools with low performance rates and serves as a member of P.U.R.E (PROPEL. UPLIFT. RENEW and ELEVATE), an organization designed to impact community through mentorship, counseling, development, and building both people and property. Dr. Gibson is also a Collaborative Partner with the Raleigh Police Department for Community Relations, a proud brother of Alpha Phi Alpha Fraternity, Inc, proud member of the Wake Missionary Association, and the General Baptist State Convention of North Carolina.

Dr. Gibson is also the proud co-author of *"Mind Over Matter"*, an anthology dealing with mental health awareness, released during COVID-19 in 2021. He has conducted workshop and seminars across North Carolina, Maryland, and Virginia, discussing the topic of mental health. The effectiveness of Dr. Gibson's presentations comes directly from his doctoral dissertation, *"Developing A Model Program Designed to Address the Stigma of Depression Concerning Pastors in the African American Church."*

Dr. Gibson is the loving husband to Margo Rice Gibson and the proud father of four sons: the late Mark Thomas Gibson, II; Lamont Junious (Atlanta, GA); Myles Tyler and Matthew Trenton ("Trent") and one daughter, Chelsey. He is also the proud grandfather of three grandsons, Malachi Joshua, and Taylor Valentine; and one granddaughter, Nola Grace.

As the visionary author of this compilation, **Suffering While Serving,** Dr. Gibson strives to share some of the countless voices of ministry leaders and their journeys to answer their call while maintaining their personal well-beings.

Bleeding While Leading

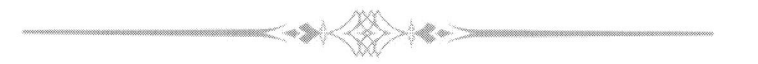

Jesus said to His Disciples *"This is my **blood** of the covenant, which is poured out for many for the forgiveness of sins."* (Matthew 26: 28)

There are some wounds that are visible to others as well as yourself, which warrant our immediate attention because of the profuse bloodshed, and then there are other wounds and bleeding that go undetected and often untreated. Those moments of unidentified hemorrhages are the focus of this chapter for your consideration. Pools of blood that gather within individuals cause not only physical issues, but also emotional damage that many suffer from, especially those in leadership. Is it possible to bleed and lead at the same time? While it may be manageable to accomplish, is it effective and healthy for the leader and those who are being led?

The average human body has roughly ten pints of blood (approximately 8% of your body weight). When one makes a blood donation, there is approximately 1 pint taken from the donor (10%); however, the body has an amazing function and capacity to replace the cells and fluids lost. The timing of that complete restoration takes four to eight weeks to replace all the blood cells extracted. When there is a severe depletion of blood, other bodily operations either malfunction or terminate altogether.

I Know It Was the Blood

One of the favorite Hymns sung in every Baptist Church on Communion Sundays across this country, "I know it was the blood for me." Growing up in Washington, DC, I heard songs about blood in church, taught in Sunday School about blood, and every Easter season watched The Ten Commandments and saw depictions of the blood in the Nile as well as over the door posts. I often wondered what was so significant about blood in the scriptures. I knew Christ had shed blood for sinners, but why was it so important for this concept to be drilled into our hearts and minds? As a moment of transparency, when I was a child, I hated seeing blood. I especially did not take too kindly to seeing my own blood coming out of me.

Whenever I was injured playing a sport of falling from a bicycle, I never looked down to see how bad the injury was...I just learned to "suck it up" and keep moving. It was these types of behaviors, along with not wanting to be seen as "soft" in my neighborhood, that caused me to ignore the seriousness of my wounds as a child. I learned to internalize my pain and bleeding even as an adult; therefore, it was an action that I normalized when trauma confronted me. Showing pain around my friends was an immediate target for being picked on and pushed around, so even if there was a significant injury coupled with excruciating pain, I would never show signs of hurt or needing help.

As I reflect on my childhood upbringing, I recall one of the famous statements often said in many households in my neighborhood "What happens in this house, stays in this house!" What a revelation to how I would respond to pain by internalizing trauma and drama to mask the true feelings that I would endure. I knew I was bleeding; I could feel the fluid running down either my leg or arms, but simply refused to acknowledge there was something abnormal about my condition. I pushed through the pain because I did not want others to see my abnormality. I was hurt, yet I hid my suffering and continued participating to save my reputation. I could not count how many times I heard older males say to me "Don't you cry, be a man, suck it up, and keep going!" The problem with those words was, I was not a man. I was a male, but still a boy who had a right to express my hurt and pain; however, to please the expectations of others, I learned to mask and conceal my true feelings for the sake of image. Blood gushing while I was still going forward as though nothing was wrong with me, but in turmoil internally. I never recognized the blood, so I was never prepared for the barriers that it would cause. What caused it…I know it was the blood!

The Blood Still Works

Now that I realized that I was bleeding, I also needed to figure out WHY I was bleeding. It all points to the carelessness of my decisions and actions, that caused so much pain, trauma, and distress. The notion that I was invincible, and I could recover from any bodily damage was just a prolonged fib I was convinced was a sheer reality. As much as held back the tears from rolling down my face, there would ultimately come a time when every situation that I refused to address would knock on the front door of my life and refuse to leave until I answered.

I grew up in a middle-class family in Washington, DC. My father was a successful self-employed contractor with plenty of governmental contracts. My mother was an outstanding educator (my kindergarten teacher) and a claims agent for a popular Insurance Company, and ultimately a Federal Government employee. There were five sons born to this union, my twin brother Paul and I were the youngest. Our parents were born during the Depression, so they taught us the lessons of hard work and making the best out of life's circumstances. NOTHING was given to us, if we wanted something for ourselves, we would work for it. We were given lectures by our father about hustling to earn our way just as he did. Life, on the surface and for the public, was pretty good for the Gibson household but underneath the clothing of life, there was bleeding. My parents divorced in 1973, and the injuries would begin for me along with the bleeding. How could this happen? What would my friends think since my dad was no longer going to be in the house? So, I did what I was taught by the streets and even from him…I swallowed my hurt and hid my wounds, refusing to seek help for the bleeding. I just kept moving through life because I still had more blood in me than what was coming out of me. I taught myself to survive and stretch through this chaotic period. I would never allow anyone to see me sweat over this devastating period in my life.

When the Bleeding is Not Blood

As my life evolved, I found myself very apprehensive about my ability to confront devastating issues that would arise. I mastered the art of camouflage to conceal the true pain and disappointment that I had experienced. Therefore, I'd become an actor who would slip into character once I was on the stage called life. Masking became my default. I was an Oscar-winning performer when it came to covering up the misery in my life, especially the trauma to my emotions and mentality.

I had experienced the loss of my twin brother and it left a gaping hole in my entire personality. His loss cost me more emotional blood than I care to remember or relive! How could God allow this to happen to me? I questioned how a God who loves those who serve Him, would allow such a tragedy happen to my brother who ALWAYS was at church and to me, who spent all my life involved in ministry. Was this the reward for serving? What a kick in the gut this was to me, and honestly, didn't appreciate the outcome for the sacrifice that had been made by the Gibson family. So, with my stiff upper lip, I kept my tears in check and smiled through my pain, *bleeding!* Looking at the image of me in a casket, I acted as though this was what God's Will was for me and my family. However, on the inside, I had a raging storm brewing!

I later would experience a failed marriage that devastated so many and left my sons in a retreated place emotionally because their mom and dad were no longer together. I began to see spots of blood on their demeanor and even their interactions with others. All this happened while an Ordained Elder in the church. "Really God…REALLY?" Serving the Savior and suffering severely in a place called *silence*. Questions were swirling all through my head, one of which was, what will be the next shoe to drop? How much more bleeding could I tolerate before fainting from these dangerously low blood levels? I continued to press on, in spite of realizing that my emotional and spiritual person was now going into shock.

Did I mention that while transitioning into the divorce, I was pastoring my very first church? What an impression that was leaving on my congregation and my pastorate. There were those who left the church and refused to return, others who remained with a critical eye on the leader, and then there were those who simply supported me, yet had no idea how to treat my wounds because of the hidden identity of who I was and what I felt. I would stand for the next few years in my pulpit, Sunday after Sunday with a clergy robe on and puddles of emotional and spiritual blood pooling at my feet. No one noticed how profuse the leakage was because they were focused on the charismatic delivery of sermon after sermon. My life was an absolute mess, and I had no one to blame but myself. I refused help, in the past, so it became a standard procedure for not just my life, but now my ministry.

I had a vision of improving what was an aged building, with construction flaws and unattended maintenance issues. However, it was ironic that I sought to correct the structural bleeding of an edifice, but was ignoring the personal hemorrhaging I was suffering from. I guess it is true, one always knows how to help everyone but themselves.

I would remain at the first assignment for thirteen years, and during that time, I would remarry and relocate from Virginia to North Carolina. I would later move from a rural church to an urban setting, where I felt I could get a fresh start and simply let the blood dry and eventually disappear. Was this God's way of trying to make up for the wounds I had already endured and were still open sores in my spirit? I would have assumed so, but when my coming was a total shock to the new congregation, I felt a stream of blood pour from my spirit and emotions.

My arrival was a shock to the very folks, in the congregation, who I was expected to support, counsel, marry, bury, christen, baptize, preach, and teach. They were rejecting me because they did not know that I was coming, nor did they have a voice in my selection. Imagine overhearing conversations, as I walked into the meeting, of some saying, "What are they doing here tonight? This is a family meeting (church conference to many) and they are NOT family!" As my heart raced, more blood pumped out of the huge gash that was affixed in my heart. I remember saying to myself, "They did not tell these folks that I was coming!" I resigned my post, at an assignment I had been at for thirteen years, and the new church congregation had no heads up that I was being brought in to succeed the founding pastor because of health challenges. I recognized the pools of blood beginning to form beneath my feet. It felt all too familiar for me, so I did what I was taught to do well…hide it, conceal it, ignore it, and move on from it!

I would eventually lead a church that was struggling with enrollment and finances back into a viable ministry designed to make an impact within the community in which we were located. While these efforts and actions were both impactful and rewarding, they were also challenging and daunting. I was wounded attempting to save a wounded and hemorrhaging ministry. Therefore, I would make the sacrifice of bleeding for the greater cause and seek no help for the emotional and spiritual wounds I had sustained. Bleeding Pastors bleed on people without knowing the significant blood loss of the leader. That was exactly what I experienced while I began to serve the people of my new assignment with a smile to mask the bloody pain of my past injuries.

The Bandages for the Bleeding

After years of enduring the suffering and ignoring the obvious pain that I was experiencing, I succumbed to the reality that I was not well. I became so bitter with myself that I submitted my letter of resignation to my new church. I wanted nothing to do with ministry, congregants, work, family…life! My prayer, each night, was to not see the light of the next day. I experienced an Elijah moment when he felt it was better to be dead than to keep living in the mental pool of blood that he sat in. I was exhausted from *faking it until I could make it*. The daunting task of leading people to Christ was no longer a priority because I was running in the opposite direction.

My blood was infecting my effectiveness to make a difference in the lives of others, I could not hear from God because I was spiritually distracted by my pain. I thought remaining busy would bandage the wounds I was suffering from, yet I realized that *activity* does not equate with *productivity*. I was moving yet I was still standing still in puddles of blood, and eventually, the stains began to show through my clothes. It was recognized and I was rushed to Triage by a group of folks who refused to empower my dysfunctional behavior. They literally initiated an intervention without my invitation and forced me into the presence of a therapist who would allow me to be Mark, not Pastor, Doctor, Reverend, Elder…just Mark! He bandaged my emotional and spiritual wounds, and he allowed me to scream and cry about what was really hurting me.

Therapy was the very care that I needed, even though that is taboo in the black church, it was the wound care that I needed to allow me to live and declare that The Blood still works. I was reminded that Christ's blood was shed so that we would be able to lead others to Him. This walk with Christ will not be without suffering or sustaining some bleeding, but just remember that there is a Balm in Gilead and that *balm* is not the cream or ointment to spread, but the ability to say I am hurting and need help. Find your hope in reaching out to a professional that can care for your wounds. It's okay not to be okay!

Chapter 5

Minister Janice Hawkins

Minister Janice Hawkins

A North Carolina native, Janice Hawkins is a minister, teacher, and writer. The daughter of the late Raymond and Annie Powers, she gave her life to the Lord at an early age and has since found many ways to serve and share the message of God's love in her local church and community. Currently, she uses her gifts and talents in service as a member of Redeeming Love Missionary Baptist Church in Raleigh, N.C., serving as Sunday School Superintendent, and Liaison for the Christian Education and Drama Ministries.

Janice is the widow of the late Joseph Hawkins, and a mother to 2 adult children, Melanie Hawkins, and Monique Davis. She is also the spiritual mother to Denise Lytle. Following her husband's passing in 2019, she released her first book, "Which Road Will We Take". This release examines and explores the many detours that we face in life. It was written to help us understand that the success we achieve begins with knowledge of the paths we are designed and created to take and the awareness that God has a perfectly designed path for every step of our journey.

Janice pursued post-secondary education with studies in English at Meredith College in Raleigh, N.C., and later received her Paralegal Degree from Kaplan College in Chicago, Illinois. Dedicated to the study of The Word, she has completed several courses on New Testament Studies at the Distance Education Baptist Missionary Association Theological Seminary, including the New Testament Survey in Jacksonville, Texas. She is also a recipient of the Christian Leaders Institute Christian Leaders Award in Spring Lake, Michigan.

Janice comes from a family of musicians and singers and has been a long-time member of United Cadence, a local gospel singing group, that has ministered at various venues across the southern US.

Janice believes in the wholeness of the gift of salvation, Christ's redemption, and His promise of eternal life. Her heart's desire is that others will receive Jesus Christ as their Lord, and use their gifts to serve Him. She lives her life with gratitude and expectation that God's best is still yet to come.

Wounded

Undoubtedly, most of us are familiar with getting some type of wound from time to time. We experience them from childhood on into adulthood. During our younger years, we learn to recover quickly because we are so eager to rejoin the activity that caused the incident to begin with, and we can join our friends or family again. After all, it was simply an indicator that we were fully present or engaged in an activity.

Surface wounds scientifically heal quickly, if taken care of properly. Soon the only residue may be a gentle reminder on the skin that is different than the other surrounding areas. However, if they are not properly attended to it may become infected, and the wound goes deeper beneath the skin and may require medical attention, no matter how minor it may have been originally. This is exactly what happened to me.

Sure, I knew the wound was there as I had felt the bleeding, and even noticed signs of infection. Yet, I chose to continue with my routines as if it would magically disappear. I tried to continue with my ministry also, avoiding the realness of my pain. Life had begun to serve me with dramatic and traumatic events.

SHIFT FROM JOY TO GRIEF

Let me explain the cause of my wounds. My mom passed away in March 2005; four months later, my middle eldest brother in July 2005. Less than a year later my baby brother passed, in April 2006. Less than a year later, my dad was called home in March 2007, and in August 2009, my oldest brother was gone too. From a thriving family of 7 down to 2, my sister and me. I barely mourned the loss of one without facing another loss. The joy of belonging to such a loving family was now replaced with grief and mourning.

Suddenly, I was trying to understand why all of this had happened, and having to face the challenge of understanding the difference between a wound and a scar spiritually. My conversation with God drastically changed. I was not asking for directions on what to present to His people, for Sunday School, in music, or the next religious production, but more than ever, WHY? WHY? WHY?

My personality of enjoying the opportunity to serve was redirected to suffering while ministering. The more I suffered, the less I wanted to serve. After all, how could I present the word of faith and hope, when I felt hopeless and defeated? So, I pulled away from God. It was when I pulled away that the Lord allowed me to see that my grief had become an infectious disease spiritually. The disease of disappointment and anger had taken up residence within my heart. How could God let this happen? Since He is so merciful and so kind, why is it that my sister and I are the only 2 of 7 that remain? And why should I want to continue in ministry, when my disappointment in His decisions was so real? After all, the ministry is closely connected to assisting others to overcome their struggles, with God at the helm.

It was during these moments of stillness and defiance, that God showed me who I was, but greater than that WHO He IS! The spirit of God manifested Himself as never before in my life. The more I tried to dodge Him, the stronger His presence became.

FROM GRIEF TO DISAPPOINTMENT

Let me just say to anyone reading this chapter, that the order of following God is all about process. No one is exempt, though everyone has freedom of choice. God now presented me with a choice. Not just a mediocre decision, but one that would change my life forever, IF I would dare go through the process to be delivered from being wounded to healing, with only a scar remaining. In other words, with the right choice, all I would have left is the residue of what HE WOULD BRING ME THROUGH. The Process!!

It was after my father passed that the healing process began. My father was the kindest, sweetest man in the world, at least to me. He was a wonderful father, a devoted husband, and one of the best musicians of his time. He was known throughout the state, and beyond. He made music flow like the lyrics of a prolific writer. To me, nothing could ever take that pain away, BUT God Showed Up.

Amid a time of ever-flowing tears, He spoke and said, "I Love you! It was His hands that carried me, and it will be His hand that continues to carry me". Yes, I felt His presence, but grief had broken my heart, and my response was a question, "How can you say you love me when all I am feeling is pain? I was honest with God, I AM DISAPPOINTED!!!!

But God is merciful, but He also knows we have our limits. He knew I was at my breaking point, and I was bleeding from the infections that were being exposed! When I turned my attention to Him about myself, I then realized I was severely wounded. The things that I had gone through were still very present in my life, and I had to face it all. Grief had left a massive scar in my life, and the disappointment that I had in God needed to be dealt with.

It is so true; confession is good for the soul. With confession, I willingly gave over to the process God had for me. The first of God's prescriptions was the revelation that I needed Him. I needed to come clean before Him so that my wound could be fully exposed. That was painful as the more He revealed, I could then see the depth of my infection. With His loving arms opened, I was afforded the choice to allow Him to wash me with His cleansing power. Just as humans sometimes do not like the sting of alcohol, the discomfort of His appearance is real. But with each step, I was reminded that I could not heal myself and that I did not, nor will I ever, hold all the solutions, He does! He is God and is stronger than I. He holds the power of who He is and awaits our letting Him in to resolve the matter. I needed major surgery for the sickness that grief had brought, and His blood, not my own, began to heal my wounds.

FROM DISAPPOINTMENT TO ANGER

Acknowledging where I was in relation to God, exposed even more about my true emotion, and the head-on collision became present in 2007 when my husband became ill. Again, my attention had to be given to someone other than myself. Blow after blow, Lord, I am ANGRY!!! This is just not fair. Let me say also, the Lord's process is not "fair". He's God and He does what He wants, when He wants, how He wants, and it is not a commandment that His actions be labeled as "fair".

God has broken me down from the inside out. Yet, at the same time, He was strengthening me beyond my wildest imagination and/or stretching my faith to the point of having no limits. Only I did not know it! Soon, with such great need of Him, I sought Him, even with the anger still inside.

Then God used the passion of one of His gifts to me and said, "Pick up your paper and pin". Understanding that I needed help, I did it. I returned to writing, just as I did when I was younger. Only now, the words had a purpose, they were purposed for me. The more I prayed, the more I was inspired to write, with each word, I could release my emotions, including the anger and disappointments I had with God. On some occasions, I would write until my tears just flowed like the rushing current of the sea. I was being healed and didn't even recognize it! Through my paper and pen and many one-on-one therapy sessions, God was healing me.

Again, the PROCESS! It was happening, God was restoring me, delivering me, healing me, inspiring me, and setting me up to be able to help someone else, not out of hearsay, but by relational experience. He HELPED me to Overcome and in the fullness of time, I was no longer disappointed or angry. God took those painful emotions away and left only a scar. He turned my grief into a time of celebration and turned the celebrations into a rejuvenated desire to please Him.

FROM WOUNDED TO CONQUEROR

Some may want not to even have the remnant of a wound, but for me it was necessary. Why? Because in 2019, my husband went home to be with the Lord. But the birthing of "the peace of God" was revealing itself in my life. Let me not leave the impression that this wasn't difficult, challenging, or even sad, because it indeed was, and sometimes still is. But the process that God had already taken me through, had changed me. I no longer had to understand, no longer did I feel the need to question God, no longer did I harbor resentment; I had received the gift of peace. I was coming into the understanding that His ways are not like my ways, His thoughts are not like mine or yours. He knows what is best for not only us but those who He chooses to take home. He really does see our beginning and our end. He really does know the number of our days, and HE really does know how to strengthen us to be better servants to the things that He is calling us to! GOD IS GOD, and GOD DOES LOVE US! We don't have to understand, but we do need His peace. Receiving peace is a process, and each individual process is specifically designed by God Himself. It's custom-made.

Now, I am thankful for the Process, and I am eternally indebted to Him for being patient with me, and not changing His mind about my purpose, even though for a season, I did not understand.

Serving is not easy, but that is because life is not always easy. But, with Him and because of His grace, the impact of the scar reminds me that I should always trust in His Will! I should always trust in His Way. The wound reminds me that HE is the WAY, the TRUTH, and the LIGHT. With the scar, I can trust God to complete that which He has purposed for me. I cannot thank Him enough for His Grace!

Chapter 6

Elder LaFonza M. Koger

Elder LaFonza M. Koger

Elder LaFonza M. Koger is truly a man after God's own heart. Married to his beautiful wife, Nyree V. Koger, together they have three children: Whitney S. Poole, Rakee L. Poole, and DaJonnae T. Koger and three grandchildren: Jayden L. Poole, Kaylin S. Morris, and Kehlani S. Morris.

Elder LaFonza M. Koger received his bachelor's in business administration from Old Dominion University in 1989 and currently works at Vann York Honda as a Finance Director.

Elder Koger presides at Bethel Way Church of Christ, Inc. He preached his initial sermon, *I Won't Take Nothing for My Journey Now,* on October 8, 2000, and was ordained an Elder in June 2001 under the leader of Apostle Joseph Adams. He owes a lot to Apostle Joseph's foundation and training.

Elder Koger is currently serving as Elder, Chairman, and Teacher of the Adult Sunday School Class and Chairman of the Audio/Video Department at Bethel Way under the leadership of Pastor, Bishop John A. Campbell, Jr.

I Had to Go Through Something

I must start by saying that *for all have sinned and come short of the glory of God.* Romans 3:23 but let me also say, *if we confess our sins, He is faithful and just to forgive us our sins, and to cleanse us from all unrighteousness.* 1 John 1:9.

There have been many times when we have said I would never do that until we did that which we said we would not do. Also, being a person of faith, it's even harder when we make a mistake. Mistake is defined by dictionary.com as "an error in action, calculation, opinion, or judgment caused by poor reasoning, carelessness, or insufficient knowledge". But what happens when that mistake becomes a sin? The enemy attacks us where and when we are the weakest. He does not come after you with something you don't like; he confronts you with something you do like. It's like he and his imps have a dossier on you. There are some things the enemy can come at you with, and you would not have a problem resisting because you never struggled or were tempted by those things. However, all of us have that one thing that as soon as it comes our way, we get weak in the knees. And just to make this clear, it's not always sexual.

The question is not about what caused you to fall, but more about what you did to get back up? You can either wallow around in self-pity or you can get up and realize that you can do all things through Christ who strengthens you. You can have a "woe is me" party or you can realize that you are more than a conqueror because you have God on your side. Steve Harvey put it this way, and I quote— "when something hits you, just don't lay there and quit because nothing in life is permanent unless you allow it". The road to recovery starts with self-forgiveness and sometimes this is a hard thing to do. We must remember that Jesus Christ took all our sins to the cross on Calvary and if He is willing to forgive us, we should be willing to forgive ourselves.

So, with that being said, there is something I want to share with you, and I hope that someone who is reading this will find the courage and strength to understand that you can *suffer while serving*. Yet, be encouraged. Know that although you go through a battle, whether self-inflicted or not, if you don't quit, you can come out victorious!! I once posed a question in a sermon I preached, and that question was- "Why does it seem your most vicious attacks come after one of your most rewarding victories?"

I was working for a local car dealership and had been there for several years and had advanced from Sales to become a Finance Manager. Then, the opportunity to become Sales Manager and run the store was offered to me. I felt like every time I turned around God was blessing me! First, being promoted to Store Manager. Secondly, being the first African American to hold the position. I was like, "Wow!! God is really doing this for me. Do I really deserve this?" There was a part of me that felt like I deserved the promotion because I worked hard, and they saw leadership qualities in me. I was proud of my accomplishments; my family was proud of me and so was my church family. I was on the mountain top and then suddenly my whole world came crashing down!

Visualize. One minute I am the one everyone is looking up to, and then, in the blink of an eye, it felt like everyone is looking down on me. One minute I am all smiles and feeling like I am on top of the world; then, in less than 24 hours, it felt like the world was on top of me! Visualize once again. I am managing the sales staff of one of the top-selling automotive brands in the world. I have just built a new home. I am married to a beautiful woman who I often refer to as my "smoking-hot wife". And did I mention, I am an ordained Elder at my church! Then, the blow hits, and hits hard! I find myself entangled in a harassment case because Delilah, as I will call her, decided that she wanted to make a quick dollar and set her eyes on me! Remember, as I told you earlier, Satan doesn't tempt you with what you don't like.

Protect What You Hear

So, faith comes from hearing, and hearing by the word of Christ. Romans 10:17 NASB.

I tell my Sunday School class that I teach this scripture because we must protect what we hear. Everybody who smiles in your face is not always happy for you. Everyone who pats you on the back is not for you. Here is the one that got me: *sweet nothings coming from the wrong person can be detrimental to our well-being.* Yeah, it may be all the things you want to hear, but just because it sounds good doesn't mean you should listen. It's been said that women like compliments, but can I let you in on a secret—men do too! It's just unfortunate for me that the compliments were coming from a woman who was not my wife. I'm not exactly sure of the time frame or how this even started, but it happened. There is nothing like hearing how good you look, or being asked, "Have you been working out?" However, when it's not coming from your spouse, sweet nothings should be just that—nothing.

Satan is crafty and he is good at his craft, but we should be good at ours, too. So many times, I have asked myself, "Why? Why did I listen? Why did I allow myself to fall into this trap? Was this a test and I failed? Was I not prepared for this test? Would I get a do-over? What were my coworkers going to think? What was my family going to think? What was my church family going to think? Was my wife going to leave me? Would I be put out of the church?

Protecting what we hear is not always as easy as it sounds (no pun intended). There are so many conversations we have through the course of a day, and according to some sources, we speak on average about 6000-7000 words a day. We should make the most of what we say and avoid getting entangled in vain conversations. Many times, we don't know the impact of what we say and even more so, the impact of what we hear. Some words tend to resonate in our mind like a marinade on a steak. However, unlike a marinade, the longer the wrong conversation resonates, it tends to spoil and not enhance. If what we hear doesn't make us better, then why do we listen?

Where's The Oil?

If my people, which are called by my name, shall humble themselves, and pray, and seek my face, and turn from their wicked ways; then will I hear from heaven, and will forgive their sin, and will heal their land. 2 Chronicles 7:14 KJV

Approximately eight years ago, I was at work and the day was going along as normal; but little did I know what was about to happen to me. I am talking to some coworkers, and I went to say something to Delilah about her performance and tardiness. At that time everything seemed to be okay; then the next thing I know, I am being told she has gone to another manager to file a complaint against me. Delilah stated that I was being hard on her because she would not sleep with me. Talk about a life-shattering moment! The phone calls from the owners started to come in, and on the advisement of their lawyers, I was banned from the workplace; I could not come back to the place of one of my most successful victories!

There had been text messages exchanged and casual conversations at work. However, the problem there is that I should have been texting and talking to my wife. All of this happened at the place where God had blessed me to be successful, and I totally disrespected Him by doing what I knew was wrong. And I must tell you, God does not let you sin successfully!

I have always believed that if I prayed, God would answer my prayers. After all, the Bible says that if I ask in His (Jesus') name, that He would give me what I asked for, but I also realized that if it is not within the context of His will for my life, the answer will not be what I desired. I went to church that night and just prayed that all would be okay, and this nightmare would be over in the morning, but it wasn't. This nightmare was shaping up to be my reality. The next day, when I woke up from a sleepless night, I had to inform my wife of what happened the day before and what was lying ahead of us. With tears in my eyes and pain in my heart, I told her of my unfaithfulness and I knew she was hurt to the core. I did not know what her reaction would be. I braced for her response. If she had said, "Get out", I would have pleaded and begged to stay, but what grounds did I have? If she had said, "I hate you," I would have told her that her emotions were getting the best of her, but who was I to tell her how to feel? If she had said, "I want a divorce", what defense did I have to make her stay? But the words that came out of her mouth shook me to the core. She looked at me and said, "Where's the oil?" She prayed for me when I didn't have the strength to pray for myself.

There is something to be said about having a praying wife and for that I will forever love her. It takes a Godly woman to be able to do that. Next, I had to tell my Pastor and even more tears fell. I don't know what hurt more, telling him what happened or handing my license over to him. He, too, prayed for me when I couldn't pray for myself. Lastly, I had to stand before the congregation that I preached to when called on and confess my sin. *If we confess our sins, he is faithful and just to forgive us our sins, and to cleanse us from all unrighteousness* 1 John 1:9. The shame that I had brought on myself, my family, and my church was unfathomable, but they showed so much love that I couldn't believe it. Also, I had to face those who gave me this great opportunity. Through the discourse of the events that I shared with them, I could see that they were trying to find a glimmer of hope to hang onto to allow me to stay, but I could also see the hurt and disappointment as they had to let me go.

Broken To Grow

Just as a tree must be pruned to continue to grow, I too felt that I was being broken in order to grow. Jesus, at the Last Supper, did the same thing with the bread. Before the bread fulfilled its purpose, He blessed it and then He broke it! The bread was still bread, but after Jesus blessed it and broke it, its purpose changed. After being gracefully broken, I realized that everything we go through is not designed to destroy us, but to help build our character, and then our testimony is to help others. Sometimes we must go through a wilderness experience alone (just ask Jesus), but it's not for punishment, but for our development. One way that you know that you have overcome adversity is when you are able to share your story. You understand that someone may need to hear your testimony. You never know who you may be encouraging by sharing that you were once down, but you got up. And because you got up, you have experienced blessings on the other side.

We, as a people, have been told that we don't talk about these things. We, as believers in the Body of Christ, have been taught to smile and say, "I'm okay and all is well". But what if I'm not okay, and maybe just maybe, if I had talked to somebody, I wouldn't be as messed up as I am? I know I have faith. I believe in the power of prayer. There were times I battled depression because I didn't want to get out of bed some days. After days of battling with this, I had a mind-altering transformation. It was as if I heard the voice of God speak to me and say, "You are better than this!" It was Black Friday and we decided to go to Greensboro, North Carolina to shop. I put on a suit and tie, took some resumes with me, dropped my wife off to shop and I went to apply for jobs. After several visits with dealerships in the Greensboro area, I got a job offer and the only thing I had to wait for was the background check to clear. Within a month after my world came crashing down, God opened the door that at one point felt as if it was closed for good! The scripture that comes to mind when this was going on is- *But the God of all grace, who hath called us unto his eternal glory by Christ Jesus, after that ye have suffered a while, make you perfect, stablish, strengthen, settle you.* 1 Peter 5:10. God was letting me know that there was a consequence to the sin, but if I would stay faithful to Him, to my wife and to my calling, He would be there for me.

Sunday after Sunday, I would go to church, sit on the front row (which was painful in itself), support my Pastor and give God a praise every time I set foot in the sanctuary! If you want to get God's attention and confuse the enemy, then don't just praise God on the mountain top, give God a praise while you are going through the struggles! You will cause the enemy to look at you and scratch his head because he won't understand that, yeah you lost some stuff but the one thing you didn't lose is your praise!

In the midst of all of this, my father passed away and my mother informed me that he wanted me to preach his funeral, but I didn't have a license to do so. I'm like, "How much more can I go through?" Yet, I was reminded by Isaiah-

Hast thou not known? hast thou not heard, that the everlasting God, the LORD, the Creator of the ends of the earth, fainteth not, neither is weary? there is no searching of his understanding. He giveth power to the faint; and to them that have no might he increaseth strength. Even the youths shall faint and be weary, and the young men shall utterly fall: But they that wait upon the LORD shall renew their strength; they shall mount up with wings as eagles;

they shall run, and not be weary; and they shall walk, and not faint. Isaiah 40:28-31.

Because of my faithfulness and my growth, while I was broken, I was reinstated and given my license back! The first message that I preached was- "I Had to Go Through Something".

In conclusion, I want to thank God for His grace and His mercy. I want to thank my wife for her love, prayers, encouragement, and forgiveness. I want to thank my Pastor and the Ministerial Staff for their prayers, encouragement, and nonjudgmental attitude towards me. I also want to thank my church family for their continued prayers and their love shown towards me and my family.

Chapter 7

Reverend Terry D. Lee

Reverend Terry D. Lee

Reverend Terry D. Lee serves as an ordained Associate Minister at the Galilee Baptist Church, Pastoral Care Ministry, Instructor for the Men's Sunday Church School, Vacation Bible Study Instructor, and Biblical Counselor to couples.

Terry was born to the late Cornell Lee (Korean war vet) and late Alzalee P. Lee Gray in Washington D.C. He was the third of four children and was raised in his early years on the farm, where he learned how to love God and family and work hard at whatever opportunity life had to offer him. Terry first met and accepted the Lord at the age of nine and was baptized at seventeen. Terry ministered by singing in the choir, serving as Co-Director of the Outreach – Prison and Street Ministry and many other ministries and capacities. The late Rev. Dr. Eugene Weathers confirmed God's calling on Terry's life and licensed him in 1992 after his commitment and attendance at the Elijah Academy Ministerial Training for Ministers (GBC). In 2003, under the leadership of the current pastor, Rev. Dr. Lloyd T. McGriff, Rev. Lee was ordained and continued his service working with the Pastoral Care Ministry, Men's Ministry, and the Director of the "Walking in Oneness Couples Ministry" for fifteen-plus years. They helped develop a six-week pre-marriage class that the church continues to implement. Reverend Lee and his wife had an opportunity to go on a two-week mission trip to Mississippi to teach Vacation Bible School with another couple.

Reverend Lee is also an Addiction Counselor, serving God by helping those returning home from prison and those addicted to substances and illicit drugs, anger management, DUIs, job readiness after returning home from incarceration, and grief management. Reverend Lee attended The Computer Learning Center and earned an associate degree in computer science. He worked as a contractor for government in the District of Columbia, Maryland, and Virginia for over 27 years. Reverend Lee worked as a food service worker for the Federal Government's United States Soldiers and Airmen Home for nine years. He has been a Case Manager for the Agape Christian Counseling and Crisis Center, where he provided services to persons living with HIV/Aids. His wife and he started a nonprofit LoveLeeTears Ministry LLC, that offered biblical counseling, marriage, pre-marriage, grief, domestic violence, Christian growth, health, and wellness.

Reverend Lee is the treasurer for the Prince Georges Baptist Association, a member of the Minister's Conference of DC and Vicinity, 3rd Vice President of the National Capital Conference of Christian Education. He attended the D.C. Bible Institution, Billy Graham School of Evangelism, Southern Baptist Extension Seminary, and Maple Spring Bible College and Seminary. He received a bachelor's degree in biblical studies from Washington Bible College and Seminary in Lanham, MD, and a Masters of Divinity Degree from Samuel D. Proctor School of Divinity (VUU), Richmond, VA.

Reverend Lee is retired (he calls it graduating from kindergarten and going to the first grade in life.). He and his late wife, Reverend Sheila A. Lee, had been married for 31 years before her passing and are the proud parents of six children and eight grandchildren.

Grieving is a Process

My wife and I have a favorite scripture: Romans 12:1: *I appeal to you therefore, brothers and sisters, by the mercies of God, to present your bodies as a living sacrifice, holy and acceptable to God, which is your spiritual worship.* (NRSV) We understand that the lives given to us from the inception in our mother's wombs are to be used as a sacrifice to serve; therefore, how we live is our worship toward God, which is the highest praise. Throughout my life, I have faced tremendous traumatic events, but through it all, I strive to be that living sacrifice, acceptable to God, daily. I understand now that God had a purpose and plan for my life from the moment I was planted in my mother's womb. As time transcended, God would use me as a prayer warrior and his mouthpiece to minister to my family and this world.

The first time I experienced grief in my family was the passing of my biological father (I was 13 years old). As my sister and I stood at the coffin, I just stared, confused, not understanding what was happening and why; in my mind, all I wanted was to ask my father why he hit my mother and disowned me. Now, I will never hear it coming from his mouth. I did not know how to grieve because I never saw any of the men in my life cry; they would either leave the room or put on a stone face. I internalized it, never talked about it, or knew how to talk about it. Tim P. VanDuivendyk, DMin, in his book, *The Unwanted Gift of Grief,* talks about when a baby is born into this world and comes out of the warm womb into this world, it grieves because they are coming out of a place of warmth and comfort into unfamiliar territory. When we have something in our lives that is comfortable, and we are used to having it, when it is gone, we grieve it naturally. Jesus" wept for his friend. Grief is unwanted, yet it is a gift from God, especially when we learn our "pathways" through grief. We all grieve differently, "Think people" – live, appreciate, and mourn mainly from the reasoning pathway of the brain. Their language naturally is with facts, investigation, reasoning, linear thinking patterns, rationality, and reasoning." "Feel People" – pathway of emotions of the brain. They use happy, sad, angry, hurt, or fearful words and cry openly." "Act People" – their pathway of actions and behaviors. People around them may not know what acts people think or feel. I learned through suffering while serving that grief is the gift God uses to help us move on through life and fulfill our purpose. (the unwanted gift).

The Call to Serve

The first eulogy I performed after being licensed was for the passing of one of my uncles, who was young at the time. His wife (my aunt) had passed away about a year or so before my uncle. She died of cancer. The family asked me if I could preach my uncle's eulogy since I was newly licensed and had been called to the ministry. Preparing to preach my first eulogy was emotionally unfamiliar territory for me, vs. preaching a sermon that has been prepped and prepared and standing in front of people from the pulpit on any given day of the week, especially Sunday mornings. As a licensed minister, I am called to minister to the family and friends of loved ones who have transitioned from this side of life. While I was sitting outside the house the night before the eulogy, I had an internal process going on within me. The grief was there in my life, and like water in a sandcastle, there was more to come (Serving While Grieving).

I got ordained a few years later, under the Baptist faith, which meant I was recognized by a body of believers to have proved myself worthy, capable, and trustworthy with and to God's word. I could not only preach but now have the covering of my church to do a burial of laying to rest the body of the deceased as well, sign a license, and conduct the ceremony because my ordination credentials were at the court in D.C., Maryland, and if needed, I could get approval through the courts in Virginia and other states. Maybe five days after my ordination, my sister-in-law passed away, and I did her eulogy and burial. I had an appointment at the hospital, the next day to have reconstructed surgery done to correct a prior operation. The procedure failed and my leg was amputated within a week. *I was still called to serve.*

After my leg was amputated, it took me a couple of months for the stitches to heal and for a prosthesis to be made. Looking back now, I can still see God's hand at work. What I had to learn the hard way is that if we do not acknowledge our grief, it can lead to addiction, depression, and suicide and could destroy marriages and families. My wife, who knew me best, realized that something was wrong, so we went to see a counselor. For me, it was the first time I had ever gone to see a counselor. The counselor said that I was grieving the loss of my leg. A light came on. I had never paid attention to the word grief, especially as a "man' who had never sat in a counselor's office. The Bible talks about grief in the Old and New Testaments; many times, as I have read it, it never applied to me until now. I was newly ordained, with one and a half legs and continuing with the call on my life (serving while grieving). I remember coming back to church for the first time since losing my leg, and the people of the Galilee Baptist Church loved on me so hard it was overwhelming. And then my pastor, Rev. Dr. Lloyd T. McGriff, called me up front to do the altar prayer (I was not expecting that, but it was what I needed). This helped me while wandering around in the wilderness, going in every direction. Tim

VanDuivendyk described it as "walking through a dark tunnel only being able to reach out and feel the wall on each side; you must keep moving until you see the light at the end."

The first wedding I performed was my cousin's, who asked me if I would fulfill his ceremony, about two months after getting out of rehabilitation. I said, yes. Since I did not have my prosthesis yet, I told them that I would bring a stool, sit on it, and do the wedding. *I was serving while still grieving.*

I received my prosthesis a few weeks later and returned to work, living life to the best of my ability. People would always say, "Wow, you get around so well and always have a smile." I could not explain to people that they saw me smiling now, but they did not see the nights that I cried after having dreams that I was jogging, only to wake up in the middle of the night to be reminded of my missing leg. Grieving is a process. John 11:35 Jesus began to weep. (NRSV) One of the keys to this scripture is that Jesus allows us to see Him as the Son of God and a human, "grieving the death of his friend." (Jesus was grieving while serving.)

Jesus did not just stay in His grief; He continued to do the will of His and our "Father" amidst doubters, naysayers, and unbelievers. Jesus told them to remove the stone. He called Lazareth's name to come forth. Sometimes, even in my grief, I am still learning that I must take back control by continuing to move forward with the little strength that I have. I must hold to God's unchanging hand. I witnessed that His hand can and will hold all your sorrow, and the sun will shine again.

Balancing Service to God

My biological father, coming home from the Korean War, found that the United States did not prepare the Veterans to return to civilization after being trained basically to kill. In the fifties, jobs were complex for black men; many veterans with melanin in their skin, were trained to be cooks, truck drivers, repairmen, and others who paid minimal wage jobs. Hence, Black Veterans had to work two or three jobs to meet ends. I am not making excuses for my dad's domestic behavior. I am thankful that my mother never taught us kids to hate him. This emotional trauma damaged my mother, brother, sister, and my life, which we must live with and through for the rest of our lives.

My mother later remarried, after several years, to my stepdad, the only active "father figure" other than uncles for me and my siblings. He was suitable to and for my mother and taught me what it is to be a man as best he could. When my stepdad started having health problems later in his life, I would visit him and take him out for rides like we used to do. All he wanted to do was go into D.C. and park in the Greenway Mall parking lot in the Southeast. We talked as we watched people going about their day. One day, after we returned home, we watched television together. Then, he looked at me with a look I did not want to see and said, "Son, I want you to do my eulogy." I never told my mother about our conversations until a few days after Dad had passed.

My mother was standing at the window, just stirring out. As I entered the room, she turned to me hesitantly and said, "I do not know how to ask you this, but will you do your dad's eulogy?" I told her that Dad had already asked me. The relief on her face was priceless. I preached Dad's eulogy while "grieving" along with the family; it was only God who held me up. Two years passed and my mom was diagnosed with cancer. Similarly, we were sitting and watching TV one day and without even looking at me, she said, "I want you to do my eulogy." Mom passed *from labor to reward* a few weeks later. It was a little more challenging, but then again, God held me up. When my stepdad passed, all I knew was that I needed to be strong for my mom. The night that my mom closed her eyes for the last time, I did not know how I would react. To my amazement, I said out loud, "Momma, you made it!" We would always have conversations about the Bible and heaven, trusting and believing that we would see Jesus one day. When I did my mom's eulogy, God gave me grace again. *I was grieving while serving.*

My bride began preparing her obituary before the diagnosis of breast cancer. She had already put it in her will: who and what she wanted done for her homegoing service (she requested that I do her eulogy). She was diagnosed with breast cancer on November 11, 2021 and passed away on January 20, 2023. Just one year and two months later. What started as breast cancer was later diagnosed as Triple Negative, a more aggressive type of tumor with a faster growth rate, higher risk of metastasis, and recurrence risk. We thought, at first, we had more time by getting the chemotherapy treatments in the hope that if it did not work, we would get the breast removed. Hearing stories of survivors gave us hope. I sometimes feel that my wife knew more about the situation long before I did because she did not want me to give up hope by telling me.

I retired early from my job so that I could be there with her at her appointments and home when she finished the chemotherapy treatments. The kids gave me a break when needed, making it much more manageable. She did things like plan a family vacation on our Anniversary. I was dragging my heels because I wanted to spend time alone; just her and me. With this look in her eyes, she said to me that she wanted to take this family vacation because she did not know if she would ever get another with us. A friend of ours suggested that I get into a caregiver support group because others are going through similar situations. I now recommend that to anyone caring for a loved one.

The day of my wife's (my baby) eulogy was like no other that I had served. While you know the work your loved one has done, it is overwhelming to see the impact on full display and then realize that you will not see that person again, on this side. It is hard. This eulogy differed from my dad, mom, family, friends, or church members. My wife was there for me through it all, and now, I was having to eulogize my bride. Yet, as I walked up to the pulpit, something was very different. All I knew was that my baby was now in her resting place; we kept our vow, **Til death do us part.**

Today, it has been nine months since we laid to rest the body of my beautiful wife. I must, at times, remind myself that she has moved on to glory to rest for a while until the return of the Lord Jesus Christ. For me, writing this chapter is part of my way of dealing with my past trauma and grief. I have and am still learning that all the trauma, in my life, is not going away. I must remember to continue to tell my story to help someone else along their journey in life. When I look back over all the situations in life, I can say that God is in control, *that all things work together for good for those who love God, who are called according to his purpose.* (Rom 8:28).

I am emotional now, even as I write. It is still day-to-day, not knowing when and where grief will show up, but through it all, God continues to carry me.

Stay awake and pray that you may not come into the time of trial; the spirit indeed is willing, but the flesh is weak." **Matthew 26:41**

Chapter 8

Rev. Alphonso Lewis

Rev. Alphonso Lewis

Reverend Alphonso Lewis has been working in the mental health/human services field for the past thirty years with various agencies and programs in the Washington DC Metropolitan area. Rev. Lewis received his master's degree in human services from Lincoln University. His thesis was on the establishment of integrated programs for the dually diagnosed (mental illness/substance abuse). Rev. Lewis is presently working on his PhD in psychology. He received a certification from Sciacca Comprehensive Services, (located in New York City) in Dual Disorder Counseling (substance abuse/mental illness) in 1999. Mr. Lewis is a Certified Addictions Counselor, a Licensed Clinical Professional Counselor (Maryland Board-Approved Clinical Supervisor), and a National Certified Counselor.

Rev. Lewis conducts group counseling and trainings on dual disorders, domestic violence prevention, substance abuse, sexual assault, marriage and family counseling, and individual psychotherapy. Rev. Lewis provided training on grief counseling and crisis intervention to a police/clergy response team in Washington DC. This team responded only in cases of homicide to provide services to the survivors. Rev. Lewis has served as an instructor for the Maryland Police and Correctional Training Commission's Advanced & Specialized Training Unit and conducted training on psychopathology and crisis intervention for the Prince George's County Police Department. Rev. Lewis served as the Mental Health Incident Commander for Prince George's County, Maryland, in the event of a mental health disaster as declared by the Department of Homeland Security.

Rev. Lewis served as a presenter on "Crisis Services" at the American Association of Suicidology's conference in Broomfield Colorado in April of 2005, and again in 2006 in Seattle Washington on "Disaster Mental Health Prepared-ness." He also served as the mental health technical advisor and participant in a production for the Prince George's County Public School System. This production included the Police, Fire/EMS, and Mental Health response to an "Active Shooter" on the school premises. The instructional production is used to train various school personnel on crisis response in the school system to support a coordinated response. He was featured on a PG Cable News special on "Holiday Blues and Depression" and on News 4 as a mental health technical advisor on Pedophilia.

Rev. Lewis has been recognized as having "Distinct Competence" in the areas of domestic violence and sexual assault. As the director of the Prince George's County Crisis Response System, he worked extensively with the county and municipal police departments as a first responder in these cases. Rev. Lewis has overseen the clinical intervention in domestic violence cases that have made national and international news. Rev. Lewis also served as a presenter and clinical panelist for the Prince George's County Department of Family Services' annual conference on Domestic Violence. He also provides trainings on domestic violence and sexual assault to other programs throughout the Washington DC Metropolitan area. He has also been trained at the basic, peer, and advanced level in Critical Incident Stress Management (CISM).

Rev. Lewis has been working as a private-practice psycho-therapist and marriage and family counselor for the past fifteen years. He also provides free trainings and seminars on mental illness in faith-based communities. These trainings are to underscore the stigma of mental illness within religious institutions; especially in African-American churches. Rev. Lewis currently provides faith-based therapy to a number of pastors throughout the East Coast, along with advising churches on the establishment of such programs.

The Walking Wounded

As a psychotherapist, I had the blessing of treating people for over twenty-five years. During that time, I've treated people with a multitude of ethnic, cultural, and religious backgrounds. Therapists are obligated to have an understanding and respect for perspectives that differ from their own. We are required to be knowledge-able and create an environment where the people we treat feel free to operate in transparency.

Depending upon an individual's preconceived understanding of therapy, the experience can be sought out with excitement, or seemingly forced into it with tremendous hesitation. Therapy has been described as a necessary entity to help individuals achieve the highest levels of emotional freedom and healing. It has also been viewed as taboo by individuals who have a notion that therapy is only for the weak.

I have some patients who simply cannot wait to have their sessions because it gives them an opportunity to have a space in their lives that's just about them! I have some people who say that therapy is the only place where they get to be human, sad, hopeful, and anxious, all without feeling judged.

It usually takes just a few sessions before most of my patients feel a sense of comfort and even a family-like environment when they start their therapeutic journey. It is usually an experience that most say was worth the time and money they invested. After all, therapy really is an investment in oneself. At the end of the therapeutic alliance, most say that they are better for having engaged in a process that quite literally, has saved the lives of some of my patients.

I wish I could say that the process was simple for everyone that I treat. I can't. That is because of the myriad of people that I treat, there is none more complicated than the Christian or preacher or anyone else in the church; except the pastor. Wait a minute, there is one that is even more difficult. THAT IS THE PASTOR OF THE BLACK CHURCH!

The taboo about African Americans seeking mental health has been well documented in numerous scientific journals. Most African Americans, over forty years old, probably have some familiarity with this stigma. The stigma alone is the number one reason that many of my African American patients tell me why they waited so long. It is the question of, "What will people think about me if they knew I went to see a therapist".

African Americans have been socialized to the mindset that seeking a therapist is something that strong people don't do. When I ask most why they waited so long, the answer is almost always the same; "I don't want people to think that I'm crazy". It is because of this stigma and socialization, that I have to use the first few sessions to normalize therapy, and to try to break the stigma!

I had heard so many pastors jokingly say, "When you pastor a church full of Black folk, you better make sure you have a good therapist!". This statement is actually a double au tundra. It is both a joke and the highest level of truth for some pastors! Not the part about being a pastor of African Americans requiring the need for a therapist. It's the part about being a pastor and needing a therapist that is so true!

Let's look at the reality of what pastor's face. Firstly, pastors are as human as anyone else in the church. Pastors have difficulty with their children, problems in their marriages, and difficulties with their finances. They have unresolved pain from their childhoods. They feel pain when they lose loved ones like everyone else. They suffer job loss, foreclosures, and repossessions like everyone else.

Pastors go through divorces; they have physical and emotional ailments and physical pains, like everyone else. Pastors feel insecure, suffer from poor self-esteem, and have a need for validation, like everyone else. Pastors feel sad and overwhelmed and hopeless and helpless and yes, worthless, just like everyone else. If there is a vocation that has a greater need for a therapist to be part of its support system, I have yet to see it!

About thirteen years ago, I went through a period of time when I lost one of the most important people in my life. She was my pastor. She was a role model, a mother-figure, and an amazing woman. Her ministry helped turn my life around, as I'm sure that I was heading to an early death. Shortly after her death, I went through a separation and then a divorce that caused me to enter into a depression. This was a very dark place in my life.

I thought I was doing things the "Christ Way", yet I was experiencing the type of depression that my patients told me about. I lost almost thirty-five pounds. I was wearing extra-large clothes on a body frame that was now a medium. I didn't see it. I couldn't feel it. I couldn't feel anything. I was trying to understand how my life could be in such a terrible place when I thought I was doing all that I could to evoke God's highest level of blessings.

During the immediate period after the separation, I would eat maybe three meals a week. When I say meals, I mean one or two bites from a sandwich and maybe a cup of coffee. My life was now on autopilot. I would get up and go to church and to work. I would make sure that my two sons had what they needed.

I was working in an inpatient psych unit. I was taking care of people with schizophrenia, depression, and bipolar disorder. I was working in my private practice. I was helping others through dark places in their lives. I was helping couples to keep their families together. I was preaching the gospel. I was trying to help my sons navigate their paths to a new way of life.

During this time, I had to file two bankruptcies. I lost my car and almost lost my home. I was trying to maintain the children's home so that they wouldn't have to change schools. I didn't want to socialize with anyone because I didn't want to invite anyone into my misery or let anyone see the shame that I was experiencing. I was a preacher, a father, a professional. **_Yet, I was the walking wounded._**

It was during this time that I took my youngest son to see his therapist. During one of the sessions, the therapist asked me, "Mr. Lewis, why don't you come in for your own session so that you can talk about how you're feeling?".

I didn't agree to make my own appointment with her. I couldn't afford to talk about any feelings that I was having because I didn't really know what I was feeling. All I knew was that I had to work full-time at the hospital and part-time in my private practice. The bankruptcy helped me to stay in the home temporarily. However, I had to pay a bankruptcy attorney. I had to make trustee payments. I had to pay my mortgage. I had to preach and teach the gospel. I had to put on a face of strength for my sons. I couldn't talk about what I was feeling. After all, I'm a therapist. I know how this goes. It's just how life is.

As I write my portion of this anthology, the Spirit of God revealed to me that the therapist asked me to talk to her because my son talked to her in his session about me! What I thought I was hiding from my son was apparently glaringly obvious to him. *I was the walking wounded.* I was the preacher/elder/

therapist who was also walking in willful neglect of just how wounded he was. After all, how do you almost stop eating and lose so much weight, yet don't notice it? It was because I was aware of my pain but was not taking care of my pain!

I eventually capitulated to seeing the therapist. I honestly can't remember all that we discussed. What I do remember is that after that first session, I was so eager to come back. During this time, I would sometimes work as many as twenty hours a day. After that first session, I was determined that nothing would keep me from coming back.

The one question the therapist asked me that began to change my life was, "Mr. Lewis. Are you telling me that you sometimes see as many as fifteen patients a day, and you don't even take a lunch break for yourself? You're not taking care of yourself". The answer was, "Yes!" My patients were telling me how much they needed their therapy and how the therapy was helping to change their lives. However, I had not realized that I had the same need for therapy.

The reality was that working was a way for me not to think about what was happening to me. It was a way for me to tell myself that God would fix me while using me to help fix others. The reality was that I didn't feel fixed. Honestly, I didn't even want to admit to myself that I was harboring resentment towards God. I didn't want to walk away from God, I was just no longer pressed to walk closer to Him.

I finally identified the emotion that was overwhelming me during this period in my life. I was experiencing indifference. If I woke up the next morning, fine. If I didn't, that would be fine too. In fact, my preference was to just wake up in the presence of God and the angels. I didn't know what to do with the pain. I wasn't suicidal at all. I just was no longer thrilled with the possibility of continuing to just exist when I was no longer living.

I continued to see my therapist on a weekly basis. I say my therapist because she is still my therapist. I was finally able to identify very powerful thoughts that would run through my mind almost daily. I shared these thoughts, and the emotions that I felt, and I began to experience release. Just like Sampson's hair began to grow while he was blinded and enslaved, my joy for life started to return. It wasn't because I was going to church and preaching the gospel. It was because I was talking to my therapist! The best part about my therapy sessions was that my therapist was also a minister of the gospel and was strong in the Word of God.

It was during this period in my life that God revealed the most profound reality about the life of the preacher/pastor to me. It was then that He revealed to me that like Hosea and his prostitute wife, He wanted me to know just how much His preachers/pastors were hurting. He wanted me to know what it was like to have the calling of the preacher/pastor, but also the unique pain that the preacher/pastor feels. He revealed that there are so many of them who are the "walking wounded." I realized that I wasn't in a one-man fraternity. There were and are so many like me.

I was now armed with a new determination. I would continue to treat those with chronic and persistent mental illnesses. I would continue to provide therapy to families. Now, I especially wanted to be a resource to the pastor, elder, bishop, and apostle and anyone else, in the church, who battles both their pain, and the stigma of getting mental health counseling.

I previously mentioned how the first few sessions are used to get beyond the stigma of treating African Americans. This is not the case with Christians that I treat; especially those in leadership who are African Americans. For them, the stigma is magnified times an infinite number! For them there is the stigma of being African American and admitting to having poor mental health. However, there is also the stigma of centuries of being told that being depressed is a demonic possession!

As I write this chapter of the anthology, I am treating pastors up and down the East Coast. It dawned on me that none of them sought out therapy because of their own epiphany. All were recommended to come and only one in Georgia started therapy after being recommended the first time. It took the others much longer to finally admit that they needed to talk to someone about their pain.

The way that I provide therapy to pastors is the same way that I provide therapy to other people that I treat who have advanced degrees or titles. I don't tell Pastor Mark Gibson that I want to talk to Rev Doctor Pastor Gibson. I tell them that "I want to talk to Mark!". This is because after so many years of providing therapy to reluctant pastors, I realize that they are used to being in a position of giving help and preaching and teaching and evangelizing, they've become lost in their titles.

The first order of business for any preacher seeking help is to let them know that they can just be their authentic selves in therapy. They can be honest about their depression. They can be honest about their feelings of inadequacy. They can be honest about how bad their marriages are. They can be honest about their indiscretions. They can be honest about feeling like God is not paying the child support to take care of them. They can even be honest about how they've contemplated walking away from the ministry. They can be honest about how they've contemplated committing suicide. They can be honest about how the stigma of a pastor admitting they are depressed has led them to believe that committing suicide is a better alternative than admitting to themselves and others that they need help because they are the "walking wounded"!

The most difficult part of providing therapy to the Black preacher is the crusty layers of stigma that have been a part of their thinking for so long. The stigma of having poor mental health while living Black. The stigma of poor mental health while preaching and pastoring while living Black. The stigma of what their church will think of them while preaching and pastoring while living Black.

It usually takes several sessions, at the beginning of therapy, for the pastors that I treat to commit to the process and become transparent. Most of them spend more time telling me that they are okay and that things aren't as bad as they are. There are numerous behaviors that people exhibit when they are having conflictual thoughts. I don't tell them about these specific behaviors at the beginning of therapy sessions because many pastors would purposely try to stop the behaviors instead of admitting just how wounded they are.

There is a saying that was popular during my mother's life in the South: "It takes a lot of hot water to pluck an old chicken". I think about this saying when I'm providing therapy to pastors/preachers because it takes so much to break through the titles and learned behavior to finally get to the real people behind the titles. Some have been masking their pain for so long that they don't even realize just how lost they have become.

My former pastor once asked me, "Deacon Lewis, what do you think is wrong with the church? Why do you think that some people just don't seem to be growing?". My answer to her then is the same answer now. It is because people in the church use the Word of God to cover up what's wrong with us. We don't use it to excavate and root out what's wrong with us. So many of us can quote scriptures from the bible in a way that would make you think we were the original authors.

Paul said, "If I would glory in anything, it would be my infirmities". So many preachers/pastors have been indoctrinated with the erroneous belief that God cares more about our availability to Him, than our commitment to ourselves to take better care of ourselves. We'll wake up in the morning with the kind of depression that makes us feel like ending it all. We'll then go to church and preach a message that will change and even save lives. We'll fellowship with each other after service and talk about how good God is. We'll then go home and once again, contemplate ending it all.

I began ministry in the church as an usher. I then went to the music ministry. Then I became a missionary. Next, I became a deacon and then a youth minister. Following that I became the youth pastor. Finally, I became a pastor. I had been active in some form of ministry for over thirty years. Since being in ministry, I have struggled with trying to have balance in my life. I can honestly say that I wasn't truly happy in my life until eleven years ago. This was after going through the process of therapy that helped me understand why I was wearing a mask for so long.

When I treat preachers/pastors, one of the first questions that I ask them is if they are happy. Most have almost the exact same answers as if they had read them in a manual. Most honestly believe that their happiness is equated to what they are doing in the ministry despite what is happening in their own lives. Most tell me how the church is growing. They tell me how many people the church has fed and how many scholarships they gave out. It's interesting how I ask them about themselves, but they respond by telling me about God and the church.

Their answers underscore a truth about so many people in ministry, and especially in the pastorate. Most of them have been lost for so long and the "walking wounded" for so long that they don't even really know what being happy looks like.

One specific pastor comes to mind. Pastor Gibson lost his identical twin brother, yet he didn't seek out therapy. He lost his oldest son and namesake in a tragic car accident, yet he didn't seek out therapy. He went through a painful divorce that impacted his relationship with his sons, yet he didn't seek out therapy. His current wife was successfully treated for both breast cancer and a stroke and yet, he didn't reach out for therapy. When Pastor Gibson had finally had enough, he didn't seek out therapy. He decided to resign his pastorate. He was angry when he woke up in the morning because God didn't answer his prayers to take him in his sleep.

I asked Pastor Gibson what he did when the doctor told him that his son had passed? He said he looked at his son and saw a trickle of blood come from his nose. He then told his ex-wife how God would make everything all right, which was after he'd prayed and asked God to spare his son's life. I asked Pastor Gibson how he grieved the death of his son and his twin brother. He couldn't initially answer the question. The reality was that he didn't grieve them. He became the "walking wounded" and put on the mask that Gestalt therapy calls "the phony-layer".

The most difficult layer that was the foundation of Pastor Gibson's belief system was that he grew up a Black man in the seventies and in one of the most dangerous areas in Washington DC. An area where a man was identified by how tough he was and by not showing emotions. Pastor Gibson knew what he was feeling, he just didn't feel safe admitting those feelings to anyone else or seeking help from someone to help process and adjudicate those feelings.

The first few sessions, with Pastor Gibson, were spent giving him permission to experience his feelings, to talk about his feelings, and to allow his tear ducts to do what God designed them to do. I told him that his tears were God's pressure-release valve. The tears are designed to help release the pain that he was feeling and that we feel. Pastor Gibson admitted to what so many of us in ministry feel and believe. He expressed his belief that Black men from his era and in that area of the city where he came from don't talk about or show their emotions. And they definitely don't cry.

It was during the initial sessions of providing therapy to Pastor Gibson, that I remembered that first day in *my* therapist's office. No one before had ever asked me how I felt about the things that I'd experienced in life. The pain, the poverty, the sexual abuse. What it felt like being the smartest person in elementary school, yet not being able to attend the first part of my graduation because my mother's welfare check had to be cashed that morning. It came early morning, she cashed it, bought me a suit. Then, I went to the second part of the graduation.

I opened up to Pastor Gibson about the pain of my life, as we were the same age, and I was from the most dangerous part of the city when DC was called "the murder capital of the country". Pastor Gibson needed a place to feel safe, permission to cry, and a hug!

I would love to say that Pastor Gibson and Pastor Lewis are anomalies. The truth is that we are not! Each time I treat a preacher/pastor, I remember that day in my therapist's office when the tears flowed so hard that I thought I was going to flood her office. Pastor Gibson found out that he was also part of a fraternity of those who are the "walking wounded", and not a fraternity of one. He later found out that there are a number of us in the fraternity. He would go on to get his Doctorate in Ministry with a dissertation that focused on mental health in the church.

So many Christians don't seek help because of the number of stigmas that continue to exist in our society. So many of the preachers/pastors that I treat talk about their pain while looking down at the floor. They find it hard to make eye contact with me because of the difficulty of accessing their pain and talking about it to another Christian who also happens to be a therapist and retired pastor.

It is very easy for the person I treat who has schizophrenia and bipolar disorder to talk about their delusions, hallucinations, the voices they hear, and their manic and depressed states. So many otherwise faithful spouses tell me about their sexual indiscretions. The drug addicts and alcoholics tell me about how they prostitute themselves to get money to buy drugs and alcohol. The women who have been sexually abused tell me about how they were brutalized and how some of them feel guilty because they believe they contributed to it. They seek help because they've decided that they don't want to hurt anymore.

It is the preacher, the usher, the missionary, the deacon/deaconess, and the pastor who sit in church Sunday-after-Sunday with their masks on. These are the "walking wounded" who continue to believe that it's better to suffer in silence than to admit that they are saved but sad. They are anointed but anxious. These are those who preach a gospel of hope and life on Sunday morning yet live a life of hopelessness and even have suicidal thoughts daily.

It is to you that I write this chapter of the anthology. Don't let shame or pride or anything else get in your way of reaching out for help. Jesus said that He came so that we can have abundant life. That includes your mental health.

Chapter 9

Dr. Gregory K. Moss

Dr. Gregory K. Moss

Dr. Gregory K. Moss, Sr., is an accomplished leader with domestic and international experience in pastoral effectiveness, global missions, and denominational educational fields. With a proven track record in utilizing his strengths of innovation, imagination, and inspiration, he is transforming lives with the love of Jesus Christ through Christian witness and relationship development.

Some of his key accomplishments extend from having served as Interim Executive Secretary and former President of the Lott Carey Foreign Mission Society, where he led efforts to build wells in Kenya and other third-world countries, ensuring resources for clean, drinkable water. He also assisted in the further development of schools in India. Dr. Moss also has been instrumental in building houses in Haiti, and affordable housing in Charlotte, North Carolina. He continues to come alongside, addressing needs and restoration following national disasters around the world.

Dr. Moss is the former President of the General Baptist State Convention of North Carolina, comprised of more than one-half million Missionary Baptist members, and known as one of the nation's premier state conventions due to its passion for missions, the earnestness of fellowship, and tradition for education. He currently serves the convention as a member of the Executive Committee and the General Board and as an advocate for convention causes.

Dr. Moss is the Faith Facilitator for the 3rd Reconstruction Federation, a community-based organization dedicated to advancing the causes of African Americans in North Carolina. Dr. Moss has served as an adjunct professor for Hood Theological Seminary, Shaw University, and Barber Scotia College. He is an accomplished consultant and leader in church revitalization, conflict management pastoral searches, leadership development, and political campaign strategies. Dr. Moss has also authored several published articles and sermons.

With more than forty years of pastoral experience, Dr. Moss served as Senior Pastor of the St. Paul Baptist Church, Charlotte, North Carolina for 17 years, and presently serves as the Principal Preacher of Chappell Memorial Baptist Church, also of Charlotte, North Carolina. He is the proud father of Gregory K. Moss, Jr., Esquire.

A Triple Storm

During my earlier ministry, I had the privilege of driving Dr. Gardner C. Taylor to and from a conference. Amazed at his ability to preach without a manuscript and paint pictures with words, I inquired how he developed the skill. He explained that reading was the key and essential. An avid reader, apart from theology, history, and classical works of preachers like Chalmers and Spurgeon, Dr. Taylor read novels, claiming they help to capture narrative in text. The exchange ignited something in me. I began to read novels, expanding my ability to grasp narratives, and learned to preach confidently without a manuscript. It effectively changed my approach to the gospel and how I approach ministry.

From that encounter, my creativity was awakened. I discovered new and refreshing ways to present the gospel through proclamation and action. For me, storytelling is essential. People remember stories and Jesus expertly used them (parables) in his teachings. The same element is contained in other media, like plays, poems, movies, and songs. Scripture is relevant to all aspects of life.

I share the above for several reasons. I am convinced that the unlocking of my creativity and my encounter with Dr. Taylor have defined my approach to ministry. It gave me the confidence to engage with my congregations in authentic and genuine ways. Confidence to not try to be, nor pattern myself after my pastor, other mentors, or colleagues. I was free to be me. Resulting in lifelong relationships, and exciting, vibrant ministry in churches I was fortunate to serve.

LIVING A CHARMED LIFE

Reflecting, I identify with Job. In the beginning, everything was coming up roses for Job. He was a leading citizen in Uz. He was admired and respected. He was wealthy even in accordance with today's standards. He had a wife and ten children. Servants galore. Land as far as the eye could see. He was devout and loved God. Things were going exceptionally well in his life. Like Job, it appeared my ministry was on cruise control- one that I did not set, nor have control over. Everything fell into place. There were a few lows. And the highs were plentiful, frequent, and steady.

Then there was an abrupt turn. For Job, the turn came in the form of an agreement between God and Satan regarding Job's faithfulness when challenged. With God's permissive will, the spirit of evil tested Job. Livestock gone. Servants gone. Ten children gone. And eventually, Job's personal health was attacked. However, in all this, though challenged to the hilt, though questioning why, Job remained faithful. Like Job, things for me took a turn. I too was challenged in ways I had not anticipated. And when the turn came, it came in threes for me.

I have heard good and bad things come in threes. There is a Latin phrase, *Omne Trium Perfectum*, meaning everything that comes in threes is perfect. The rule of three is based on the idea that humans process information through pattern recognition. It is the smallest number that allows us to recognize a pattern in a set. Hat tricks, trilogies, and tricycles (three wheels) come in threes. Human personality- ego, id, and super-ego come in threes. Trio, three-piece suit, trimester in pregnancy comes in threes. There are three-legged stools, three sides of a triangle, three feet in a yard. There was Goldilocks and the Three Bears, The Three Little Pigs, and the Three Stooges. Satan tempted Jesus three times in the wilderness, Peter denied Jesus three times, there were three crosses on Calvary, and Jesus was in the grave three days.

Through the years, I witnessed colleagues who experienced difficult pastorates. Often, it appeared they were "climbing the rough side of the mountain." Whether fault lay with them or the church, it appeared there was ample church hurt to go around. They experienced constant conflict, frequent skirmishes and tension with church officers and congregants. They were discouraged, unhappy, unfulfilled, and fed up. They were anxious to leave, find a new opportunity, desired a change of venue. And on some occasions, unwilling to change their own position and ways, and tired of butting heads with a "we shall not be moved" attitude, several gave up on pastoral ministry altogether.

However, not so for me. I was extremely humbly fortunate, in that throughout my pastoral career, I had a minimum of the aforementioned problems. I was blessed to be yoked to congregations that were patient and willing to bend and flex with me, as I matured as a pastor. By the grace of God, they, by and large, followed my leadership. Albeit, I am convinced it was partly due to spending sufficient time building relation-ships that have withstood the test of time.

Like Job, things had gone well for me. The first twenty years of my ministry were a beautiful journey. They were exhilarating, exciting, and some might say, effective. It was faithful, fruitful, and fulfilling. And it was fun and satisfying. Yet, like many of my colleagues, I never envisioned becoming a pastor. I had my sights set on being a surgeon. Pastoral ministry was the last thing on my mind. Then God called, changed my agenda, and I landed in seminary rather than medical school. Now, without a doubt, I know doing ministry and mission are my passions. There is nothing like walking in your calling and working in your passion. When you work in your passion, you are not concerned about accolades, rewards, or even getting paid. You would do it for free.

THE THREE D'S

Like Job, things took a turn for me, challenging me in ways I had not anticipated. When the turn occurred, it arrived in threes. It was a triple storm. A series of events I label as the three D's: Divorce, Divorce, and Death. Unlike Job, it was not sudden. It was not quicker than right now, nor sooner than at once. It was deliberate, slow, and gradual, but no less destructive, debilitating, and devastating. What was once a smooth, joyful, uninhibited ride on the highways and byways of ministerial life, was now wrought with blind curves, steep hills, and deep valleys. Obstacles appeared out of nowhere. As much as I preached faith and trust in God, when faced with this triple storm, I knew I had failed miserably.

Over the years, I have witnessed great paradigm shifts relating to church life and expectations regarding the life of a pastor. In the eyes of congregants in the Black Church, the pastor was held in high esteem. In the minds of some, he was one step from God. As a pastor, you were expected to uphold a certain image: clean-cut, dressed to the nines, drive a decent car, live in the "right" neighborhood. And it was preferred you would be married. Unfortunately, the expectation of being married caused many pastors to marry, not because of love and compatibility. They made the poor decision of marrying to get and or keep a church. They married to uphold an unrealistic image. They married to please people who themselves were not authentic; people who left no room for grace. All that mattered was keeping up appearances. Never mind if the pastoral couple was suffering, unhappy, unfulfilled, and unsatisfied because they bought into an unsustainable, unhealthy lifestyle for the sake of leading a church.

THE SCARLET LETTER

My first church surprisingly called me as a young, green, inexperienced, still wet-behind-the-ears, single man to become pastor. Though not unheard of, it was not the typical practice of most Baptist congregations. They were wonderful people who gave me room to make mistakes as both a pastor and a young, single man. However, though initially, singleness was not problematic, there were subtle hints and pressures regarding the church's personal preferences about my marital status. Their subtleness, aided and abetted by the more overt opinion of my pastor/mentor, and my desire to neither displease nor embarrass the congregation or my mentor, was enough to nudge me into marriage.

The marriage lasted for fifteen years. And as with all marriages, there were ups and downs. I do not, nor will I at any point have a disparaging word to say about my first spouse. Together we were given a beautiful gift in our son, who is now grown, married, contributing to society, and enjoying his life. And we both enjoy his love and support, and he ours. Notwithstanding, my wife and I grew apart in ways that were not healthy for us personally, which had the potential to affect my interaction with the church. I can, however, speak of my shortcomings and own the blame that is mine.

I got it twisted. My immaturity as a pastor and as a man was prominently responsible for my failure in the marriage. The flow chart that guided my pastorate and family looked like this: God-Church-Family. However, after divorce and serious reflection, I confess I was essentially married to the church. Not even to God. To the church. Most of my time and focus was on the church. Not my spouse, not my son, nor even my own self-care. It was the church. It was from the ashes of my marriage I learned a hard, valuable truth, I had it all wrong. My flow chart should have read, God-Family-Church. I was out of order and paid a harsh price.

I was cultivated with old-school values that guided what pastors did and did not do. I remember my pastor advising me against divorce. "You should not divorce. It will damage your credibility with your present church and greatly inhibit your ability to pursue other church opportunities." I did not heed his advice. I, not without trepidation, went against my cultural grounding and the wishes of my mentor. I was extremely anxious, concerned, and worried about how divorce would affect our family and my ministerial career. Now that I wore the Scarlet Letter 'D,' what will the community say and think about me?

In the same season, an opportunity was presented to me to pastor another church in a more urban setting. Going through separation and a pending divorce hanging overhead, I did not have confidence this church or any other congregation would consider me, especially in light of the tremendous abilities, talents, and qualifications of other applicants. Despite having received information regarding my marital difficulties, I was invited to interview with the search committee. I decided to address the issue forthrightly with the search committee. I stated that during my twenty prior years of ministry, I had buried many persons, with whose families I exhibited compassion and sympathy. But it was not until my grandmother, who raised me, passed that I was better able to empathize with families who experienced the death of close loved ones. I further stated the Bible indicates Hosea too, had marital difficulties, and so do I. I ended by saying pastors do not board in Heaven and live on earth. We experience what we live and preach about.

STRIKE TWO

I was called to serve at the church and divorced while there. The church was supportive, and with cooperation, building relationships, and through faith, we experienced an incredible season of growth; spiritually and numerically. During my tenure, another D reared its head. My mother passed. It was a dark time for me. Although my grandmother was my primary parent, I loved my mother. I assumed a role reversal and became her primary caretaker. I had no idea how deeply affected I was. I kept pouring myself into ministry.

It was during this low period I entered a romantic relationship which led to my second marriage. Like before, not recognizing I was neither emotionally nor spiritually healthy, I made decisions that negatively affected me and those in my sphere of influence. Looking back, I was overextended. Pastoring a large, urban church, being president of a 500,000-plus member church state convention, a vice-president of a global mission society, a community activist, a political advocate, and a plethora of other responsibilities, and now I was becoming a spouse again.

Prior to marrying for the second time, I failed to listen to my gut, my confidants, or heed warning signs. They warned, "BRIDGE IS OUT!" My failure to heed the warning was indicative that something was wrong with my decision-making. A scant sixteen months later, I was on the doorstep of divorce-again! The church offered grace, but I had entered a bleak season on my journey, plunging and spiraling into a deep, dark abyss, and negatively affecting family, friends, and church. Although functioning pastorally, anger and isolation became my food. The words of Smokey Robinson's song, "Tears of a Clown," nailed my posture.

THE GRIM REAPER

A few years later, while recovering from surgery, I was notified of the death of my pastor and mentor. He had been the only father I ever knew. The news was devastating! A mutual friend and I, along with others, watched demise infringe itself upon him. We begged him to retire, to enjoy the fruit of his labor. It was painful to watch what had been the tremendous career of a visionary leader, a people's champion, a pastor's pastor, gradually fade to black. Though I could not attend his homegoing, relatives made it possible for me to spend a quiet hour with him at the mortuary to pay respects and say goodbye. And three days later, my godson died from a gunshot wound. Like body blows, depression descended and changed my life forever.

Early on a Sunday morning, the triple storm manifested itself in the form of my not being able to raise my hands above my chest. I, unbeknown to others, was teetering while standing. With God's grace, I preached and immediately made an appointment to see my doctor. Upon examination, he surmised I was totally exhausted and manically depressed, both affecting my physical health. He asked me what has become one of the most important questions of my life, "Do you want to live? If so, let it go" (referring to the pastorate). I was not ready. Stepping away from my passion and love (church, preaching, ministry), had been the farthest thing from my mind. Yet, I heeded his advice. I chose to live! My doctor recommended a psychiatrist, who in turn recommended a therapist. They became my dream team, and I am convinced because of their intervention, I am alive today. I am currently continuing my relationship with my therapist; looking forward to every session.

The stigma regarding Black clergy seeking psychiatric assistance has robbed many colleagues of a path to a healthy, productive existence. Depression, among other mental illnesses, without intervention, ruins lives and potentially leads to death. God has provided professionals who are called and skilled, to come alongside us, when mental care is needed. As important as it is to invest in physical and spiritual health, it is equally important to invest in mental health. Therefore, I urge clergy, pastors, and ministry caregivers, to "get on the couch." It is an important part of self-care and could mean the difference between life and death. I sincerely hope you choose to live. I did!

Chapter 10

Pastor Johnnie Randolph, Jr

Pastor Johnnie Randolph, Jr

Pastor Johnnie J. Randolph, Jr., is a dedicated servant of God and an inspiring leader in the community. Since July 1, 2020, he has been serving as the senior pastor at Mount Zion United Methodist Church – Magothy, a vibrant congregation located in Pasadena, Maryland.

His journey of faith began in a life-changing moment in 2012 when Johnnie surrendered himself to Jesus Christ, setting the course for his spiritual calling. He has been an integral member of Queens Chapel United Methodist Church (QCUMC) since September 2008, where he actively participated in various roles within the church community.

With a heart full of compassion and a deep-rooted faith, Johnnie's devotion to service has been evident through his active involvement while at Queens Chapel. Over the years, he served as an usher, choir member, and a valuable member of the QCUMC stewardship committee. Additionally, he held significant responsibilities as chairperson/member of the QCUMC Staff Pastor Parish Relations Committee, Certified Lay Minister, Lay Servant, and Lay Leader. His dedication to the United Methodist Men's Unit at QCUMC is exemplified by his life membership.

In addition to his spiritual calling, Pastor Randolph has a passion for education and holds an associate degree in science from Excelsior College, along with a Bachelor of Science in Health Sciences degree from Trident University International. Furthermore, he is enrolled in the Wesley Theological Seminary Course of Study, furthering his knowledge and commitment to his ministry.

Beyond his career and spiritual journey, Pastor Randolph served the nation proudly in the U.S. Army for more than 23 years, retiring with the rank of Master Sergeant (E-8). Following his military career, he continued to serve as a Medical Technologist at the Department of the Army Civilian, retiring after 19 years.

His commitment to studying the Word of God, teaching bible study, and sharing the Good News of Jesus Christ through preaching remains unwavering. One of his cherished scriptures is the 23rd Psalm, which serves as a constant source of inspiration and strength.

Pastor Johnnie J. Randolph, Jr., is not only a devoted spiritual leader but also a loving family man. He is happily married to Yolanda (Lonnie) Lanaux-Randolph, and together they have raised a beautiful family. They are blessed with three adult children, Johnnie III (deceased), Tanya Jones-Austin, and Lakiesha Randolph-Richardson. The couple also takes great joy in their five grandchildren and three great-grandchildren.

With a heart full of compassion, a deep-rooted faith, and a wealth of life experience, Pastor Johnnie J. Randolph, Jr., continues to touch the lives of many through his ministry, spreading the message of hope, love, and the unwavering strength found in Christ.

To connect with Pastor Randolph:
Facebook: @Johnnie J. Randolph Jr.
Email: johnnie.randolph@verizon.net

I Waited

As I think about my story and the things I've been through, I often *suffered in silence* and wasn't sure I would make it through. However, I can stand today to say that I've met, and know someone who brought me through my personal storms in life. That person friends, is Jesus!!

I'm going to begin my story by sharing a few events that shaped who I am today. The first two turned out with me being in the right places at the wrong time. I say that to say that during those experiences, I was not physically harmed but I was harmed psychologically.

The first occurrence was seeing a childhood friend shot in the chest in the parking lot of our high school. We were just hanging out minding our own business and someone showed up to settle a dispute with my friend. The way he settled the dispute was to shoot my friend in the chest, fortunately, he did not die.

The second occurrence was during my first duty assignment, which was in Germany, I was 19 years old at the time. There was a day when a few friends and I were hanging out in the recreation room, playing pool. We suddenly heard a female's loud scream coming from the stairwell of the barracks.

Next thing I knew, my fellow brothers-in-arms and I witnessed what we thought was a fistfight. One soldier was on the floor with another standing over him with arms flailing. We approached the two with the intent of breaking up the fight, but we quickly realized the soldier standing over the other had a knife in his hand. The soldier on the floor was being stabbed repeatedly. When the assailant eventually stopped the stabbing, he was taken into custody while some of the other soldiers and I ran to our respective rooms and grabbed our first aid kits. We began to apply direct pressure to the victim's wounds. I happened to be applying pressure to a chest wound, causing me to be close to my friend's face. He seemed to be going in and out of consciousness. At one point, the young man looked at me and said, "Get me a priest, I just saw the devil!" My friend lost his life on that day.

After that incident, I began having nightmares, unable to get a good night's sleep. I waited to seek or speak to anyone about what I saw or heard; yes, I waited. This happened around 1976. I waited until 2009 before I ever spoke to a therapist about this experience. Why did I wait? I waited because I could not lose face with the other soldiers. I could not allow myself to appear weak, so I waited.

A few of the older soldiers advised that I would be able to get some sleep if I had a few drinks before going to bed. I took their advice. I did sleep or perhaps, I should say the alcohol slept. The drinking led me to acquire an addiction to alcohol. I began dabbling in illicit drugs because I did not know where to turn. So, I waited, although I did not know what or why I was waiting…I just waited.

Along the way, the military became my chosen career; thus, I remained in the military for more than 23 years. Then, one Christmas morning, while serving outside the continental United States, my family and I were enjoying Christmas morning and my mother called.

My mom called to let me know that my father had passed from this life to the next. I knew he was ill. I had spoken to him on Thanksgiving Day. I'll never forget the words he shared with me during our conversation. His words were, "Son, don't worry about me, I'll be home for Christmas." So, it was as he said, on that Christmas morning, he made his way to his heavenly home. Of course, my way of dealing with the pain of his passing was to drink, to ease the pain. That was Christmas Day, 1990. I never spoke to anyone about the emotion I felt, and I must admit that Christmas has not been the same since my father's passing. I did not speak to anyone about it, I simply waited.

Admittedly, during the times that I just shared, I was not a true believer in Jesus Christ, I knew "of" Jesus, but I did not "*know*" Him.

The same holds true when my brother died unexpectedly. I had the unfortunate occurrence of being present at his home and then at the hospital when he died. Here I was, caught up in another season of waiting; while my brother was in the emergency room; waiting to hear how my only brother would be. I felt as if my brother had died at his home while I was there watching, as paramedics worked to save him. He was rushed, by ambulance, to a local hospital. And as I recall, I didn't pray.

WOW, I'm now ashamed to say, I just waited, I didn't even pray... my God, my GOD!!! As I'm writing a song, these words come to mind... *couldn't hear nobody pray, couldn't hear nobody pray, way down yonder all by myself, I couldn't hear nobody pray.* All I knew to do was wait. Not long after my brother's arrival at the emergency room, a doctor came from the back, looked at me, and said, "Your brother is brain dead, what are his last wishes." I was shocked! I cried (privately). Then, I got myself together as I was charged with the responsibility of calling my mother. So, I called and advised her that her eldest son, my only brother, had died. I suppose one can imagine how that conversation went. And, yes, you guessed it, I waited… for what, I do not know. I just waited and called on my old friend, alcohol to ease my pain. That was the year 2000. I never spoke to anyone about that experience. I just waited.

Along the way, I went through a nasty divorce. A few years later, in 2002, I married my current wife. Everything seemed to be going well. Then, in 2004, we received the news that my wife had been diagnosed with breast cancer.

WAITING THROUGH TRAGEDY

Then on September 9, 2005, my only son, along with his best friend, were murdered. Many people wanted to know what happened. I would say it was like something one might read about in the newspaper and think it will never happen to them!

The short version of what happened was, my daughter and son-in-law were going through a divorce. The young man, my former son-in-law, decided midstream that he no longer wanted the divorce. However, my daughter was adamant that the divorce was necessary and she would be going through with it. He, her estranged husband, became enraged and threatened to kill my daughter; and if he could not kill her, he would kill the people she loved the most. One day, my former son-in-law and an accomplice showed up at the home of my ex-wife. My son and his best friend were there babysitting my granddaughter (my daughter's daughter) and the daughter of one of my daughter's friends, they were taken hostage. A little later, my daughter's girlfriend arrives and she too was taken hostage.

I received a phone call from my daughter telling me what was happening. I live in Maryland; my children live in Alabama. When I received the call, I happened to be on the golf course that afternoon. I imagined things would end peacefully, although I did send up a prayer. So, I waited for God to answer my prayer, I prayed for my son, my grandchild, and the other hostages to be returned unharmed. I waited… as the minutes turned to hours, I began to become more concerned. All I could do was wait, so, I waited. It was about eight hours later, a little after midnight, on September 9, 2005, that I received a call.

I was expecting to be told that my one and only son, his good friend, my grandchild, and the other hostages had been rescued. However, that was not the case. I was told that my son and his good friend had both been murdered. Fortunately, the other hostages had been rescued.

BROKEN

I cried, I wanted answers, my heart was broken, I was confused, my heart had been pierced. My brokenness turned to anger, not just toward the murderer. I was angry with God for not answering my prayer, I considered it to be a simple prayer to answer. I felt as if I too died on that day; having been stabbed with the entire blade of the knife, into the deepest chamber of my heart, and remaining there.

Thus, in my brokenness, I began a trek through a season of unimaginable pain and hopelessness. And of course, as I waited, I called on my old friend, alcohol.

OH, YOU OF LITTLE FAITH

What little faith I did have waivered. I began to wonder if there was a God and if so, how could a good and loving God allow something like this to happen? So, I waited, not knowing what I was waiting for! I did not tell anyone how I felt. I did not seek counseling. I just did the best that I knew to do to survive while in a place of hopelessness. The only thing that I knew to do, while I waited, was to drink as I was suffering in silence.

THE LIGHT WAS TURNED OFF, I WALKED THROUGH THE VALLEY OF THE SHADOW OF DEATH

I fell into a state of hopelessness, drinking more than ever, no one to talk to nor did I know how to come out of the dark pit I had fallen into. This description best describes how I felt at the time. It was as if someone crawled into my ear, made their way into my brain, and turned the light switch off. And no matter how hard I tried, no matter where I looked, I could not find the switch, to turn the light back on.

I became suicidal. The pain was excruciating and I no longer felt like living. I came to a point where I would take my pistol and bullets and place them on the dining room table. The pistol on my right side and bullets on my left, both sitting on the table. With my old friend, alcohol.

I would hear voices, of good and evil, the evil voice telling me to kill myself, if I did, the pain would go away. Yet, I would hear another voice telling me not to do such a God-awful thing. I felt as if I was losing my mind!! One day, I fell to my knees and prayed.

In November 2009, I went to the emergency room of a local hospital. I explained to whomever it was at the reception desk, "My brain is not working right, something is wrong with my brain, I need to talk to somebody!" I was able to speak to a psychologist who advised me that I should spend some time in the psychiatric unit. Three days to be exact, I complied. Which is where I met my therapist and psychiatrist.

After three days and refusing medication, I was released. The drinking did not stop, it got progressively worse. I should say I became a master of disguise. I was a functional alcoholic, able to hold a job, did well. I received an award and promotions, even as I was in the deepest valley, I had ever been in. I was meeting regularly with my therapist, yet I continued to get worse. I eventually, in 2010, I decided, on the advice of my therapist, to attend a psychiatric partial hospitalization program (PHP). While attending PHP, I decided to start psychotropic medication, I accepted the fact that I was an alcoholic. I stopped drinking cold turkey on May 1, 2010.

I KEPT GOING TO CHURCH

In 2008, I joined a local church, I kept going to church. And when service ended, I did not want to leave. I felt the need to sit in the sanctuary, where I felt a sense of peace. I just wanted to sit and wait even though I did not know what I was waiting for. I eventually served on different ministries and began to sing in a few choirs. Then something miraculous happened!!

MY LIGHT CAME BACK ON!!

One Sunday morning in 2012, I don't remember the month, I don't remember the day, nor do I remember the hour. All I remember is hearing the preacher preaching and the choir singing. The pastor opened the doors of the church and I found myself walking down the aisle. That is when I surrendered my life to Jesus Christ. From that point forward, the trajectory of my life changed. I started attending Bible study and eventually began leading the study.

Jesus called me to the ministry. I served as a certified lay minister, then God called me into pastoral ministry. Before I answered that call, I prayed for about 90 days. Then, the Lord spoke to me, saying, "Johnnie, everything I allowed you to go through has prepared you for a time such as this." Here I am today, pastoring a local church and doing my best to lead others to become disciples of Jesus Christ. I teach them to forgive, to love, and encourage everyone to seek and find Jesus.

OH! Lest I forget, the hatred and vengeance I once harbored in my heart are no more. I learned to forgive the young man for murdering my son, although I still expect that he should be held accountable for his sin. My studies have revealed to me what the Bible says, which is, vengeance is God's, not mine!

See friends, a songwriter once said, "create in me a new heart." And it is through the power of the Holy Spirit it can become a reality. God's Word says, in Ezekiel 36:26, *I will give you a new heart and put a new spirit in you; I will remove from you your heart of stone and give you a heart of flesh.*

I share my journey to encourage you, so that if or when you find yourself in darkness, if your light begins to dim, or your light goes out, you too can wait on Jesus! Jesus Christ is the way, the truth, the life, and *The Light*!

I now know who I was waiting for all those years! It was Jesus. He restored my soul. He turned my light back on. Look friends, If He did it for me, He can do it for you!! Can somebody say, AMEN!!

Chapter 11

Rev. Lillie I. Sanders

Rev. Lillie I. Sanders

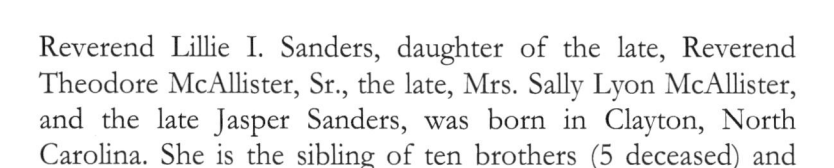

Reverend Lillie I. Sanders, daughter of the late, Reverend Theodore McAllister, Sr., the late, Mrs. Sally Lyon McAllister, and the late Jasper Sanders, was born in Clayton, North Carolina. She is the sibling of ten brothers (5 deceased) and seven sisters.

She cast her lot with Watts Chapel Missionary Baptist Church, Raleigh, North Carolina as an associate minister in November 2009, under the pastorate of the Reverend Dr. Harry L. White, Jr. Reverend Sanders relocated to the Greater Raleigh area in August 2009 after serving faithfully for 30 years at Macedonia Baptist Church, Arlington, Virginia. Reverend Sanders served in the servant roles of Mission Ministry Coordinator at Macedonia Baptist Church and at the mission district levels in Northern Virginia, Old Testament Instructor, Church Librarian, and Library Ministry Coordinator at Macedonia Baptist Church, Arlington, Virginia, and as Mission Coordinator at the district level in Northern Virginia. She is a member of Delta Sigma Theta Sorority, Inc. Reverend Sanders' passion is teaching and preaching the "Word of God" that others might know God's "Word, His Will, and His Way."

Reverend Sanders received her early education in the public schools of Johnston and Wake Counties, North Carolina. She holds a bachelor's degree in social science and a Master of Arts degree in Library Science from North Carolina Central University, Durham, North Carolina, and an endorsement in elementary school administration from George Mason University, Fairfax, Virginia. She has done additional collegiate work at Catholic University, Washington, DC, and the University of Virginia, Charlottesville, Virginia.

Her religious education includes Certification in Religious Education from Virginia Union University (Evans Smith Institute), graduate studies at John Wesley Theological Seminary, Washington, D.C., and a Master of Biblical Studies degree and a Master of Divinity degree with a concentration in the Old Testament from the Maples Springs Baptist Bible College and Seminary, Capitol Heights, Maryland. In July 2006, Reverend Sanders was a participant in the Gordon-Cornwell "Preachers' Seminar", Hamilton, Massachusetts, based on *Biblical Preaching* by Haddon Robinson. This was a blessing to her preaching ministry. Reverend Sanders was ordained to the Gospel Ministry at Macedonia Baptist Church on October 25, 2006, under the pastorate of Dr. Leonard L. Hamlin, Sr.

Honors: February 2013 Black History Profile: Lillie I. Sanders --- By Lauren Ramsdell; February 21, 2013

Founder's Day Speaker --- North Carolina Central University, Durham, NC (HBCU) October 19, 2013

Reverend Sanders is a retiree of the Fairfax County Public Schools (VA) and Prince George's County Public Schools (MD).

BORN AGAIN

Reverend Lillie Sanders is born again, ordained to serve, redeemed by His blood, non-negotiable to Satan, abiding in Christ, grateful to God, about her Father's business, insured through the Cross, and will never turn back.

Suffering on Purpose for a Purpose

"Eighty Going North", eighty years plus, is a blessing from God despite any suffering I have experienced. Looking in the rear-view mirror of my life allows me to "Remember, Reflect and Rejoice" in my "Suffering, on Purpose for a Purpose". From Genesis to Revelation, scripture records that there is a purpose for all God's creation and the fullness thereof. (Psalm 24:1). God ordained suffering in our lives to help achieve all His purposes for humanity. His ultimate purpose is, "To conform us to the imagine of His Son, Jesus Christ". Throughout scripture, our suffering and our purposes are "Signed, Sealed, and Delivered, from the mouth of God to the ears of His people.

REMEMBERING: Preparation for My Purpose

Because of my December birthday, I was a late starter for first grade. In first grade, Mrs. Young's teaching struck a chord in my heart that harmonized with one of the purposes God created me for – to teach.

I hit the ground running for "Excellency". This consistent "yearning and burning" to become a teacher was a lifeline that kept my God-given purpose in focus throughout my elementary, elementary, middle, high school, and college years. The desire for academic success has remained steadfast and unmovable.

During my early years, suffering via domestic violence paid a visit to my family. In that environment, there was no "Joshua Mentality"- *As for me and my house, we will serve the Lord.* My parents eventually divorced and my mother, five siblings, and I went to live with my maternal grandparents. My grandparents' home was not a "House of Chaos", but a home of Christian order.

We learned early from my grandparents' motto, "Hard work never killed anyone". My grandparents, as sharecroppers, were determined to rear us with Christian values and good work ethics. *"Start children off in the way they should go, and even when they are old, they will not turn from it."* (Proverbs 22:6 NIV). Church attendance and participation, worship, and receiving the "free gift" of salvation were not an option. Over the years, those Christian values and good work ethics have paid high dividends in every area of my life.

Church ministry training and my grandparents' expectations of good grades increased my yearning to escape the sharecropper life and become a teacher. Our teachers had an open invitation to drop by our home with any behavioral or educational concerns regarding my siblings and me. Sharecropping played its role; it could "draw you" or "drive you"! It drove me to be more determined to "chart my course" in pursuit of a career in teaching.

I had three aunts who graduated from high school in 1952. My grandparents wanted them to attend Howard University in Washington, DC. My grandfather had arranged for them to live with his sister. To my surprise, my aunts, seven years my senior, declined the opportunity. I was appalled. Shame on them! This made me more determined than ever to pursue my calling to teach.

The love for reading has always motivated me to learn and keep on learning. My oldest sister and I were in the same grade. As sharecroppers, we had to miss days out of school for farm labor and to launder clothes for the family. Through it all, I was determined to excel academically, for I had a "dream"! Like Mary McLeod Bethune who studied by the moonlight, I used a flashlight to study by if my homework was not finished by my grandparents' "lights out" curfew. My sister often, jokingly, reminds me of this.

While excited about school and learning, I had to compete with the discriminatory mentality of "fair-skin and good hair" – a slavery tactic embraced by some teachers and many students. In eighth grade, I won a writing contest that was to yield a photography session. I had to beg the sponsoring teacher to take my picture. The picture was finally taken. In conversation with a classmate, whom I had not seen since high school graduation (over 60 years), she reminded me of how another classmate and I, though academically successful, were often overlooked.

My high school principal once said to my brother, "I heard that your sister, Lillie, wants to attend North Carolina College at Durham, but she will never make it". While these comments made me sad momentarily, I had a "dream" and I was determined to "show Mr. Principal, better than I could tell him!" Negative words can wound! Yet, the solution lies in what we do with such negativism. Turn it into something positive? I did!

REFLECTING: Determination in My Purpose

A delay is not a denial became my inspiration. With no money to attend college, my dream of becoming a teacher could not "die". I relied on my faith, through Jesus Christ, believing that "nothing is too hard for God." Available scholarships were given to "hand-picked" college-bound students. There was a small scholarship no one wanted. I asked for it. I was not "too proud to beg". After receiving it, I was still unable to begin college with my graduating class.

In those days, my sharecropper grandparents felt that if they got you through high school, they had fulfilled their duty. With no money available for college, I had to "plan my work and work my plan". I took a job as a housekeeper/children sitter, saved what money I could, and prayerfully applied for the National Defense Loan for the second semester, February 1960.

At Christmas time, December 1959, several of my high school classmates, who went to North Carolina College at Durham, (now North Carolina Central University) came home for Christmas break and visited me. They excitedly shared about college life. They engaged in a conversation concerning something that happened in the recreation center. They used the word "Rec" and I thought that someone had been involved in a "wreck". I asked, "Who was in a wreck?" Well, the house went up in laughter! I was wounded and embarrassed. I was more determined than ever to fulfill my purpose – to become a teacher.

While my dream was deferred and no money was available, Mr. William Holloway, the loan officer, may have noticed my tear-stained National Defense Loan application and felt the heartbeat of my sincere plea. God was at work! The loan was granted in January 1960.

With a two weeks' notice, I informed my employers that I was accepted for matriculation at North Carolina College beginning February 1960. In light of their planned NASCAR vacation, the husband congratulated me, but the wife responded, "Yeah, but this puts us in a hell of a predicament for childcare". My apologies, but college was calling!

I was scheduled to attend North Carolina College at Durham, (NCCU), February 1960 with a National Defense Student Loan. My meager savings covered some clothing and other minimum necessities. I reasoned that at college, I could use my cosmetology skills to make extra money. With my bags packed and $141.00 gifted from my grandparents, my grandfather and I struck out in his green Packard, bound for North Carolina College at Durham, North Carolina. Entering the campus, we were greeted by the statue of Dr. James E. Shepherd, College Founder; a fact expounded upon in a Founder's Day Address that I delivered 54 years later on the 50th year (Golden Anniversary) of my Class of 1963.

My first semester was great, in spite of normal challenges. I was proud to be on my career track and blessed to have a great uncle and aunt who lived near the college. They provided spending change when needed. Upon returning to college for my second semester, my "volunteer helping spirit", assisting the dormitory matron, landed me a job at the home of the President of North Carolina College. As one of the three student helpers, I remained in that job throughout my 3½ - year undergraduate college career. Working at the home of the College President and his wife was an honor and yielded benefits untold.

In 1960, students at A & T College, Greensboro, NC staged a sit-in at a Woolworth lunch counter that brought civil rights to the national stage. North Carolina College (NCCU), along with other colleges, immediately joined the march for civil rights. While there was no discussion with the President and his wife about my participation, I completed my daily job duties, at the President's home, and joined the civil rights evening meetings. I learned at my 60th 1963 College Class Reunion that the President of the College, Dr. Alphonso Elder, received a call from the town mayor to halt our student demonstration. Dr. Elder refused!

The owners of the farm on which my grandparents were sharecroppers saw me on television participating in the civil marches and alerted my grandparents. On a visit home, my grandparents ordered me to "cease and desist". I respectfully received their command, but upon return to campus, I continued with the "Fight for Freedom".

My college years, great as they were, soon passed and I unexpectantly finished college in 3½ years. The College Placement Bureau secured a job for me immediately. With a conditional State Department of Education certificate, I began my teaching career. I pursued my master's degree and worked in schools that qualified me for loan forgiveness in the liquidation of my National Defense Student Loan indebtedness. My journey, to this point, had experienced minimum suffering.

The workplace eventually became my real training ground for *"Suffering: On Purpose for a Purpose"*. I am sharing a few negative experiences in the workplace in the "hope" that they will encourage others to have a relationship with God and stay focused and committed to your purpose (s) for the long haul. These challenges did not take me down as my faith kept me reliant on God's promise, "*I will never leave, nor forsake you*".

- A teachers' coup was formed to falsely document my job performances to adversely work against me. (A custodial employee who overhead the coup planning warned me on the condition of anonymity.) Human Relations was called in to mediate. Prior to the Human Relations' visit, I stumbled upon a secret (after-school) meeting of my principal and teachers planning for the Human Relations' visit.) With a copy of the charges in advance, I was able to face my accuser and respond to the charges. (No charges stuck!) (Isaiah 54:17)

- A School System Evaluation Team was sent to my school with an unannounced visit scheduled for my class. Again, an angel from the team alerted me. The Holy Spirit led my class! The angel on the team shared that in their follow-up meeting, the principal on the evaluation team concluded, "I don't know what they are talking about". (Psalm 91:11-12)

Out of these experiences, the Area Superintendent and his assistant, a former coworker, met with me. I was appointed to a position (that was planned-in-house for a white male). I praised God for the new assignment. Trouble, however, greeted me with total rejection. I had already come through many dangers, toils, and snares, but now, the racism went to another level. All kinds of tactics and set-ups were planned against me, but God is a *Promise Keeper*. I saw the manifestation of God's Word, *"Touch not my anointed, do my prophet no harm"* (Psalm 105:15). Sorrowfully, the following ensued: the murder of a daughter, terminal cancer of one librarian, dysfunctional marriages, etc. Through it all, God kept me and allowed me to retire from Fairfax County Public Schools, Fairfax, Virginia.

God blessed me to get hired across the Potomac River in Prince George's County, Maryland at a predominately Black school. I was now retired with two salaries, and this caused jealousy. Solomon declared, *"There is nothing new under the sun."* Scripture reminds us, *"Fret not the ways of the evil doers for they shall soon be cut down"* (Psalm 37:4). These are a few of the many *Suffering While Serving* experiences that I encountered in the workplace. After five years, I was vested in the Prince George's School System, and I retired permanently from education with two retirement benefits. God is good.

REJOICING: Celebration of My Purpose

God intends for suffering to shape us and mold us to accomplish His purposes for humanity. His ultimate purpose is to conform me to the image of His Son, Jesus Christ. Like many new Christians, I readily sang the song... *Jesus loves me, this I know, for the Bible tells me so.* Out of this love, I believed, that life would be largely problem-free. Obviously, I had not been privy to John 16:33 where Jesus reminds us that *"in this world you will have tribulation but be of good cheer, for I have overcome the world."*

The believer's *Suffering: on Purpose for a Purpose* in Servanthood Ministry may be summed up in the words of Langston Hughes' poem, "Mother to Son". While there will always be suffering in this world, know that it lives everywhere: your house, my house, the courthouse, the schoolhouse, and yes, the Church House. Yet, our God, who calls us to a love relationship with Him, promises to never leave us alone. Through it all, scripture reminds us that, even in suffering, *"remain steadfast, unmovable, always abounding in the work of the Lord, knowing that our labor in the Lord is not in vain"* (1Cor. 15:58).

I receive *Suffering: On Purpose for a Purpose*, as God's "preparation process" for my servanthood work in Christian ministry. As I embarked on this Christian journey, I learned that there is no perfect church because you and I are a part of the membership. While we meet people, throughout the Bible, who have been blessed by God, also we meet people in the Old Testament who were killed by the sword, persecuted, and mistreated, ridiculed, stoned, chained, and imprisoned (Hebrews 11:35-38). Suffering still lives!

When Jesus stepped on the scene, He offered us His love (John 15:9), joy (John 15:11), and peace (John 14:27); yet He never promised us a life void of suffering. Despite numerous negative challenges in my life through *Suffering: on Purpose for a Purpose,* I choose to rejoice in my suffering. Suffering allowed me to learn survival skills while under stress, resilience while seeking recovery, and achievement of my God-given purposes through my problems.

As I travel, *Route 80 going North*, my *Suffering: On Purpose for a Purpose*, brings healing to my heart, peace to my soul, and compels me to, "*Love God with all my mind, heart, soul and strength and love my neighbor as myself*" (Matthews 22:37). The Giver of the Greatest Gift is worthy!

Scripture records how, on Calvary, our Savor *Suffered: On Purpose for a Purpose*, that we might have eternal life and live with Him in eternity. *He was wounded for our transgression, bruised for our iniquities, the chastisement of our peace was upon Him.* (Isaiah 53:5) If Christ, *Suffered: on Purpose for a Purpose*, why not us?

Chapter 12

Dr. Shawn Singleton

Dr. Shawn Singleton

Dr. Shawn Jerome Singleton was born on May 1, 1971, in Jamaica, Queens, New York to Thomasina Singleton. At a very young age, he moved to Sumter, South Carolina to live with his grandparents. He is united in Holy Matrimony to the former Sister Andrea M. Brown, and they are the proud parents of Jalen, Shawn II, Jacqueline, and Alaina, and the super proud grandparents of Micah Elijah Dye.

Dr. Singleton was baptized as a teenager by the late Dr. D. W. Broughton at High Hills A.M.E. Church in Dalzell, South Carolina.

He was educated in Sumter County School District #2 and is a graduate of Hillcrest High School. He has earned a Bachelor of Science in Business Administration *(Accounting)* from Elizabeth City State University, a Masters of Arts in Religion, a Masters of Religious Education, a Masters of Divinity Degree from Liberty Baptist Theological Seminary, and a Doctor of Ministry Degree *(Pastoral Leadership)* from Norfolk Theological Seminary and College.

He was commissioned as an Officer into the United States Army Military Police Corps in December 1993 as a Distinguished Military Graduate and completed his military service at the rank of Captain. He holds the distinction of being the first ROTC Cadet from a Historically Black College to be selected to the Army's All-Pro Team. He proudly served his country at various duty assignments and was highly decorated for his service, and after receiving an Honorable Discharge, he settled in Virginia with his family.

He was licensed and ordained into the ministry at Mount Gilead Missionary Baptist Church in Norfolk, Virginia; where he was under the leadership and tutelage of Dr. Shelton Murphy. While at Mount Gilead, Dr. Singleton served as the youth minister and was instrumental in launching the *Boyz 2 Men Mentoring Program*. He served as the Pastor of Bethesda Baptist Church in Virginia Beach, Virginia for six years, and the Pastor of Greater Mount Zion Baptist Church in Chesapeake, Virginia for four years. While there he was recognized by the City of Virginia Beach for launching the *Salem's Elite Mentoring Program* at Salem Middle School and the *Ocean's Elite Mentoring Program* at Ocean Lakes High School. On May 10, 2017, he was called to serve as the 16th Pastor of the historic Martin Street Baptist Church in Raleigh, North Carolina.

Dr. Singleton has been an Adjunct Professor of Biblical Studies at Norfolk Theological Seminary and College and has taught subjects ranging from Greek and Hebrew Language Skills, Church History, Old and New Testament Studies, Church Growth, and Personal Evangelism. He has traveled abroad to South Africa as a missionary and has worked on various missionary projects along the East Coast to spread the love of Jesus. He is the former Vice-President of the Norfolk Area Baptist Association, and the former Program Chairperson for the Tidewater Metro Baptist Ministers' Conference of Virginia; and has attended countless training sessions and workshops as he sought to study God's Word, so he might show himself approved.

In his short time in Raleigh, Dr. Singleton has been recognized for his transformational leadership within and outside of his church. He recently led Martin Street Baptist Church through a half-million-dollar renovation of its primary sanctuary, and with his visionary leadership, he led the church through the COVID pandemic and created an online ministry that reaches thousands of worshippers each week. Dr. Singleton has used his creativity and knowledge to assist other churches in the area to create or expand their online presence and streaming capabilities. He has been a guest lecturer at Shaw Divinity School and Apex School of Theology, a session presenter for the Wake Missionary

Baptist Association, and he is currently a member of the Benson Theological Seminary Cohort in Wake County, North Carolina.

Dr. Singleton is a Life Member of Omega Psi Phi Fraternity, Inc., the NAACP, and the Elizabeth City State University Alumni Association. He conducts seminars on marriage, church leadership, and financial management, and praying and fasting, and he has shown himself to be a wonderful preacher and teacher of the Word and likes to describe himself as *"a humble servant that has been blessed to do the Lord's work one day at a time and one step at a time."*

"There shall not any man be able to stand before thee all the days of thy life: as I was with Moses, so I will be with thee: I will not fail thee, nor forsake thee."
Joshua 1:5

Suffering in Silence

When I accepted God's call to ministry, it was crystal clear to me that God had called me to be a Pastor, and I approached this call to ministry as I had approached every new venture in my life, and that is, with an air of confidence that I was going to be great. I knew that I was the last person that most people would have expected to be called into the ministry, but I had a made-up mind that I was going to prove God right and prove everyone else wrong. I was certain that I was going to be a success in ministry.

I know some may look at that as somewhat arrogant, but I had reason to feel the way I felt, because up until that point in my life, I thought that I had the "Midas Touch," and I thought everything that I touched was going to turn to gold, and was going to turn out to be successful. I breezed through high school, as an athlete and as a student, and then I went on to breeze through college, as an athlete and as a student. Then I went on to breeze through ROTC and I even set standards that continue to stand to this day. I went on to breeze through a military career, where I was decorated for my service and I won multiple awards for exceptionalism. After I got out of the military, my civilian jobs were awesome, and I was quickly promoted on each job, and I was recruited to higher positions with other companies. So, when I entered the ministry, if anyone had asked me, I would have confidently told them that everything in my life was coming up roses, and I expected to be very successful in the ministry.

Even my entry into the ministry went well. I preached my initial sermon in front of a packed house, and the comments and the responses, from the congregation, were tremendous. I preached from Isaiah 55. My topic was, *He Is Able,* and the genesis for the message was, if God can take somebody like me, and make him a preacher, then there is no telling what God can do for you. I quickly became the youth minister at my church, and the Youth Ministry was completely on fire for the Lord. I was the youngest minister out of 20 on staff, but it was apparent that I was going places in the ministry, so I expected to start my first church, and in short order, I expected that it was going to flourish.

But oh, was I wrong...

I started my first church, and immediately I began to experience a series of personal tragedies. I lost my job, I lost my home, I lost my car, and I almost lost my hope, because the mental strain was more than I could handle at the time. I had been through tough times before but it was nothing like what I was feeling at the time, because in my mind, I was God's chosen servant, so all of this was not supposed to be happening to me!

I was stepping into the pulpit week after week with a smile on my face, but then I would spend the rest of the week in my own personal hell. I fell into the deepest state of depression, and I lost all motivation; there were times when I would lose the motivation to preach at all. When I reflect on some of the messages that I was preaching, I wasn't preaching to the choir, but I was preaching to myself. It wasn't that I was trying to encourage my members to keep on going; instead, I was searching for a way to encourage myself to keep on going.

I was following what God had called me to do, yet everything was going terribly wrong. I had no reliable income because the church could not afford to pay me a salary, I couldn't put a roof over my family's head, so we had to live with my wife's sister, and I didn't have a car to drive, so a member allowed me to use her 1996 Chevy Caprice. So many times, I would ask God to help me make sense of what was going on in my life. I would call out to God, with my eyes filled with tears, and I would say to God, "if this is what you had planned for me, I could have stayed out in the world."

And if you think that things couldn't get any worse for me, you're wrong. I ended up taking a minimum wage job as a security officer, just so I could maintain some dignity by bringing some money into the house. Then about a month after getting the job, I was hit with a letter from child support enforcement to review my child support payments. When the judge set my child support, he set it based on the salary I was making as a pharmaceutical sales rep, instead of setting it based on the minimum salary job. When I asked for an explanation, the judge told me that it wasn't my son's fault that I wanted to pursue ministry and seminary, versus wanting to pursue a higher-paying job. In his opinion, I had the qualifications to be making more money, but I had chosen to be in the ministry full-time. I tried to tell him that I didn't choose the ministry, but the ministry chose me. In an attempt to be funny, the judge said, "Then I can choose for you to pay the adjusted child support amount". In the end, I was working a full-time, minimum-wage job, and when I got my check every two weeks, I was bringing home $77.14!

If I wasn't depressed before, I was definitely depressed while I was working that job. This Pastor had completely hit rock bottom! Week after week, I had to stand in the pulpit and declare that *God is good all the time and all the time God is good*; when week after week I had to ask God why all of this had befallen me. I had to tell other people to just hold on, while I felt like letting go. I had to tell other people to trust God, while I was losing trust in God. I had to tell other people that God will answer your prayers while wondering when God was going to answer my prayers.

When I think about being at my lowest points, I am amazed at how infrequently anyone even stopped to ask me how I was doing or was I okay. People just assumed that if I was preaching every week, then I must be okay. I tried talking to a preacher friend about the fact that no one seemed to notice or care what I was personally going through, and no one seemed to notice or care how much of a struggle it was for me share the *good news* when all I was experiencing was bad news! At the end of our conversation, I really had to reexamine if being in the ministry was really for me, because what he told me just shook me to my core. He said, "Hear me young preacher, people will tell you that they love you and they care about you, but the truth about ministry is, that most people are not concerned with what you are going through or what you are dealing with Monday through Saturday. What they are really concerned about is, come 11:00 am on Sunday morning, do you have a word from the Lord? As long as you're standing flat-foot and preaching the Word, they're going to assume that you're fine, because whatever you're going through, and whatever is hurting you; is not stopping them from getting a Word." His words gave new meaning to 2 Corinthians 4:12, **So then death worketh in us, but life in you.**

I can admit that I wanted to quit the ministry. Several times I told my wife that I was going to resign, but every time I tried to resign, God would not accept my resignation. There were days that I contemplated driving somewhere that no one would know me, and just hiding out, so I could escape the pain. However, every time I tried to drive away, I found myself driving in circles. The people around me never knew how badly I was suffering mentally and emotionally, because I learned how to wear a spiritual mask, and I learned how to respond how people expected a Pastor to respond. I never contemplated suicide, but daily I would think about running away from everything and everyone.

When people ask me about being in the ministry for 20 years, I am quick to tell them that I'm not in the ministry because I wanted to be; I'm in the ministry because God wouldn't allow me to get out. It's not one of my proudest moments in life, but I had given up on the ministry, and I was tired of things not going my way. My son asked me for a video game, and I couldn't buy it, because I was flat broke. That was when I said, "That's it!" A friend offered me an opportunity to get back into pharmaceutical sales, where I could make $80,000 annually, and I told him that we'd get together on Monday.

But God!!! However, God said, not so fast my friend! That particular Saturday, I bumped into a minister at LifeWay Bookstore and he asked me about a book that I was holding, *Tough Times Never Last, But Tough People Do*. He told me that he was a Christian counselor and he invited me to sit and talk with him over lunch. I really didn't want to meet with him, but I figured it couldn't hurt because I wasn't planning to go to the Monday Minister's Meeting because in my mind, I was through with the ministry. We met that Monday and in the midst of our conversation he not only told me about several biblical characters who were called by God, but then faced great tragedies in their lives. The thing that really grabbed a whole of me was when he told me about his personal failures in the ministry, and how he felt that God used his personal failures to ultimately make him a better preacher.

The way he explained it to me made perfect sense to me, and it helped me to make sense of what I was going through. He reminded me, that *we have this treasure in earthen vessels,* but there are times in ministry, when before God can fill us up with His glory, He has to empty us of ourselves. We would continue our meetings over coffee and through those meetings, he helped me to see that if God had allowed me to be successful in ministry, I would have given myself most of the glory, because up until that point in my life, I had taken all the credit for all the good things that I had done. This Christian Counselor knew this because he would always ask me about my past successes. I thought he was always asking me about my past, so he could remind me of my successes, but eventually, he told me that he was always asking about my past successes because he was waiting to see how long I was going to continue to take all the credit. I knew he was heaven-sent when he told me that God had seen and heard how I had been stealing all His glory for all my successes. So, God was simply letting me see just how successful I would have been without Him working on my side. This fellow minister helped me to see, that God didn't want me to be unsuccessful in ministry. No, God wanted me to be very successful in ministry; but God wanted to make sure He was going to get all the credit and all the glory.

Just when I had hit rock bottom, God sent a fresh wind to lift me back up on high. I felt the spirit of God telling me that He was going to start turning my situation around. I wish that I could tell you that from that point on, everything in my life has been going well or has gone according to plan, but that would be the furthest thing from the truth. Since that time, I have experienced some of the worst moments in my life, and since that time I've had to pick myself up off the mat more times than I can count. Yet my life and my ministry have never spiraled out of control like that, again. I think the reason it hasn't is because since that time I have been more committed to focusing on my mental health, and I have been committed to talking to others about what I am going through. There was a time when I felt ashamed to tell people that I was hurting or I was depressed, but God and a whole lot of counseling have helped me to accept that I can be attacked by depression just like everyone else.

Not only do I make it a point to speak openly about my feelings with my Pastor, but I'm proud to say that I've benefited from the help of counselors. I've also benefited from having a wife with whom I can be open and honest about the triggers from my past that have the potential to lead to future bouts of depression. God has placed people around me that regularly check on me, and people that can recognize when the signs of depression are popping up in my life. I think doubt, disappointtment, and depression are the side effects of pastoral ministry, because I've never met someone who has been pastoring for any significant amount of time, and they haven't shown signs of one or all of these side effects. Knowing the side effects of ministry, and knowing that not everyone can persevere through these trials and tribulations time after time and year after year, should help church members understand why *many are called to be ministers, but only a few are called to the pastorate.* The pressure and demands for imperfect people to try and preach a perfect gospel are enough to weigh a person down. However, when you add the pressure and demands of dealing with one's own family and finances, and the pressure and demands of that come along with leading people who don't want to go anywhere; it's understandable why so many Pastors are dealing with the side effects of ministry.

I don't share everything I'm going through with my congregation, but I am much more open with my congregation about the side effects of ministry. As a result, I am much more insistent about the fact that I need time away from the church and the people, so I can recover and revive myself in order to meet the pressure and demands of ministry.

Chapter 13

Rev. Joe L. Stevenson

Rev. Joe L. Stevenson

Reverend Dr. Joe L. Stevenson is a noted theologian, academician, and prognosticator of the gospel. For over 40 years, he has carried the mantle proclaiming the death, resurrection, and ascension of Jesus Christ.

A native of Crawford, Mississippi, Dr. Stevenson first acknowledged God's anointing at an early age. In 1980, Stevenson accepted God's calling into ministry and was ordained to preach by Reverend Joe A. Stevenson of St. Joseph Baptist Church in St. Louis, Missouri.

Dr. Stevenson first pastored the Temple of Faith Missionary Baptist Church in Kansas City, Missouri for six years. During this time, he hosted a full-time Gospel radio ministry. Subsequently, he would go on to serve as pastor of New Liberty Baptist Church in Detroit, Michigan for 16 years as God blessed the ministry to grow from 500 to 1000 disciples. In 2006, Dr. Stevenson was positioned to lead Macedonia New Life Church in Raleigh, North Carolina where he proudly serves as senior pastor. He considers it to be his assignment to lead this great church in shaping the future of Christ's church. As a church planter, Dr. Stevenson and Macedonia New Life Church are nurturing Iglesia Hispana Macedonia.

In addition to Dr. Stevenson's full-time ministry at Macedonia New Life Church, he held administrative and teaching positions at the first historically Black institution of higher education in the South, Shaw University. Stevenson served as Director of Continuing Education and remains at Shaw University Divinity School as an adjunct associate professor. Stevenson has also served as an adjunct professor at Myers Taylor School of

Religion, Ashland University, and Ashland Theological Seminary. Academic courses taught by Dr. Stevenson, include *Pastoral Care, Evangelism, Church Administration, Spiritual Formation, and Social Activism, Person in Prayer and Spiritual Disciplines.* He is the 2021 recipient of the Gus Witherspoon Award in religion and a 2023 recipient of the Community Impact Award from The Northeastern Region of Sigma Gamma Rho Sorority, Inc. and The Middle Eastern Province of Kappa Alpha Psi Fraternity, Inc. In March 2023, he was appointed to serve as Director of the Black Church Leadership Academy at Shaw University.

Dr. Stevenson is committed to professional, civic, and social organizations. He is the former chairman of Friends of Detroit City Airport and a former Board Member of the Raleigh Urban League. He served as the Second Vice President of the Baptist Missions and Education (B.M.&E.) State Congress of Christian Education, Director of Ushers and as the Field Missionary for the Prospect District Association of Churches. Currently, Dr. Stevenson holds a seat on the Board of Directors for LUCC Ltd., and is a member of the Ecumenical Council, National Association for the Advancement of Colored People (NAACP), and his beloved fraternal organization, Kappa Alpha Psi Fraternity, Incorporated.

Dr. Joe Stevenson earned a Master of Divinity in Pastoral Counseling, Master of Arts, and Doctor of Ministry in Formational Counseling and Pastoral Care from Ashland Theological Seminary of Ashland University, located in Ashland, Ohio. He cites the psalmist David as a favorite biblical reference and adds, much like David, God's light gave him clarity; clarity to seek salvation and in turn, God gave him covering to sustain him throughout all facets of life. Since being selected as a mentor for the Lilly Pastors of Excellence Program in 2003, he shared this mantra to mentor pastors in their professional development for healthier congregations of Jesus Christ. Now, he continues to share the Gospel of Jesus Christ internationally. He toured the Vatican City and Ancient Rome. He has lectured and preached in Lusaka, Ndola, and Sioma, all in Zambia; and in Johannesburg, South Africa, and serves on the advisory committee for the inception of the Shikaru Leadership Academy.

Dr. Joe Stevenson and his wife, Brenda, a Wake County Public School educator, are blessed to be the proud parents of five children- three sons: LeVaughn, Joseph, and Brennan, and two daughters: Makiea & Briona. They have ten grandchildren – Khloe, Londyn, Victoria, Nora, Michelle, Joey, Kaleb, Micah, Ezra and Aalaya.

Loving and Serving God in the Off Season

"What happened to all those prayers I prayed and the ones I gave up on praying along the way? It seems always that the task before me was learning how to distinguish when it was God who seemed hidden and when it was I who was hidden, and above all, learning how to wait out the time until we found our way back to each other. Renita Weems (Listening for God)"

O Lord God of hosts, how long will you be angry with your people's prayers? You have fed them with the bread of tears and given them tears to drink in full measure. You make us an object of contention for our neighbor's, and our enemies laugh among themselves. Psalm 80:4-6

Joe, "God sent you to Kansas City for you to grow that church. God sent you to Detroit so that church could grow you. Why God sent you to Raleigh will be revealed in time." These words were spoken to me by my mother who rests with Jesus. I've experienced many highs and lows in ministry. As I reflect on the words of my mother, what has been revealed so far in this phase of my pastoral journey is that the Holy Spirit is not *only* the Great Comforter. During this time in my ministry, the Great Comforter also became known to me as the Great-Dis-comforter (Place a pin here and leave it until I say remove it). This could be characterized as a season of suffering. I take full responsibility as a catalyst and contributor to much of the suffering and the circumstances that brought me into the season in which I call, "The Off Season "of ministry in my life. I am my worst critic. Psalm 80 expresses my emotional and spiritual health during this season. There was a time during the period of which I write, when I thought God was angry with me and my tears and suffering were divine retribution.

It's difficult for me to wrap my mind around the idea of success in the ministry as many perceive success to be. For me, it was ministry in the "off-season" with minimum success; a season in which a great deal of struggle, pain, and suffering was experienced. It was also a season in which I experienced grace and mercy I never knew. I also came to know the love of God I never knew. The season I call the "off-season" was birthed when I mishandled the ministry and then tendered an unprovoked resignation letter. The fact that God continued to use me despite my actions, blows my mind!

Demonic or Divine

As a pastoral caregiver and seminary professor, I have taught many pastors the importance of knowing the difference between matters of mental and spiritual conflict. Matters that are psychotic and neurotic aren't spiritual matters. The demonic on the other hand is. It was during the off-season that I came face-to-face with all three. I also call it the off season because of the years of tears. Many tears have been shed during this season. The losses seemed to be more than the gains.

This was not my preferred season of ministry. I believe we each have a preference when it comes to seasons of the year. Some people prefer spring over summer, fall over winter. Some people wish their seasonal preference would never end. My "off-season" was what Terry Wardle calls, "The Season of God's Own Choosing." The emotional struggle and suffering; a season of God's own choosing? Really? It got so bad that for a very brief, and I mean very brief second, Satan showed me a way out. The demonic impulse attacked me mentally, and for a brief second, I wanted to end it all. With everything else going on in this season, I thought my life was under arrest and under attack. The place I saw was darkness masquerading as light. I knew God wasn't directing me into this place. Satan attacked my mental health.

I vividly recall that day with such clarity. On that day, on the front doorknob of our house, and attached to the windowpanes and on the front door, were disconnect notices from every essential utility service including cable TV. Each notice was in different vibrant colors for all the neighbors to see the pastor's lights, water, gas, and cable were shut off! At that very moment, the demonic impulse in my thought was that life had become overwhelming; I could let go! The demonization in that moment was swift. Yet more swiftly than that demonic attack; that second that seemed like an eternity, The Hand of God snatched me back from that dismal place! God snatching me back was all the confirmation I needed. It confirmed for me that this initiated a new season for me that was by God's divine design; a season of God's own choosing. Even in the off-season, God will get the glory. While serving in this season, God is teaching you how to handle the season.

While many may look upon ministry success based on apparent realities of grandeur. Is this God's way of considering what is a successful ministry?

I have had a wonderful ministry journey for approximately forty-five years. The last several years of that time in the ministry, I consider it ministry in the "off-season." My reasons for saying this are purely based on my self-assessment. I considered several factors. For example, those ministry events I no longer have access to. I no longer have full access to national audiences. The big church, big city revivals ceased. There's so much more I can say about this. Again, I digress.

The season has also revealed to me how uniquely different pastors and preachers of the gospels are. I believe we each wear a piece of God's heart. Not everyone who is a pastor will serve in those popular spaces. This revelation became vital to understanding how God continued to use me in ministry in my "off-season". It's from that place I believe God is glorified. For example, Elijah was fierce in his faith while struggling with depression. Esther was reminded of why she was brought into the Kingdom. Jeremiah was an emotional wreck; his emotional well-being was never within the margin. He cried all the time and almost quit ministry altogether. God told the prophet Hosea to marry Gomer. God told Ezekiel to not mourn the death of his wife and to continue in ministry. Job needed a therapist after suffering so much loss. Paul could not rid himself of what he considered to be a thorn even after much prayer. John the Baptist's pulpit was in the hills with locusts for his diet. Even Jesus was considered eccentric and maybe even mentally ill by his own family. I wonder if for me, this is that piece of God's heart of which I am to wear. Is this season of ministry for me, God's due season for me to minister in; a season of God's own choosing?

There will be no break in this season. For me, it's an "off-season" in ministry but I continued to serve. The season is off but not ministry. There was no sabbatical (there should have been), and no extended vacation. While there were retreats, there was a lot of pain and suffering while still serving. God has given grace to endure. Not without suffering and some struggle. Still serving though! Not all the pain was transforming, some of what I experienced was transferred to people I love and people who loved me. There are times, during this off-season, when the only sensible response for me was to self-medicate. I'll say more about this in the next book.

When Faith and Feelings Collide

The "off-season", for me, began in 2006 when I resigned as pastor from a congregation that loved me and my family deeply. I accepted the call to serve a congregation that would, in time, come to accept and love me as pastor. Neither church deserved to experience the pain of those early years of the off-season. The cause and effect of the resignation as pastor from a loving church and recognition as pastor of a loving church did not come without significant pain. While I blamed others for the cause and effect. I marvel at how God used this season of suffering so I might experience His Grace during what I caused, created, and call the "off-season". I could not have written about this many years ago.

Upon resigning, On January 1, 2006, I asked the church to release me from a 90-day transition period and accept a 30-day transition instead. My reason was that I did not want to second-guess my decision to leave. I was moving forward in faith. This is when my faith in knowing God was moving me, collided with my feelings. Within a few days of resigning, I withdrew my resignation and rescinded my acceptance to the new assignment. The news I was not leaving was met with joy and excitement by some and disapproval by others. By email, I rescinded my acceptance to the other church. It was graciously accepted with understanding and prayer.

It was an early morning call from one of the older deacons at my former church who loved and respected me as pastor. He never called me. His ministry, every Sunday, was to pin a carnation on the lapel of my suit coat or robe. He did this every Sunday for the nearly 17 years I served this church. A practice he continued from my predecessor. I remember his words the morning he called, *"Good morning brother pastor. You know I love you and you know this church loves you but if God has called you to move-it's better to obey God than man."* I replied, *"Yes sir."* Earlier I asked you to place a pin at (*These words were spoken to me by my mother at a time when the Holy Spirit, the Great Comforter became known to me also as the Great Dis-comforter*). Now take up the pin. Now I must take back my decision to stay at this church and reconnect with the church I officially withdrew my acceptance from.

This single action is what set into motion the season of God's own choosing. It was for me, the beginning of the season of serving while suffering. Not just for me, but for both congregations. The church I served for many years was grappling with why after their giving so much, I would resign. The new congregation grappling with why and how I could possibly be brought back when I had officially withdrawn my acceptance. Having to stand a second time to take it all back, cut a deeper tear in the fabric of fellowships it took years to develop. In one church, relationships were suddenly lost forever, and further widened a gap, rendering it impossible to build relationships in the other. To this day, I live with the pain of that reality. It continues to keep me awake. When feelings and faith collide, if allowed, feelings can dismantle the foundational pillar of one's faith and can lead to great suffering, but I digress.

Reconnecting with the church, where I now serve, did not come without controversy. The wisdom of the church leaders was clear to me and reaffirmed that my move to another church was God's intended plan all along. This would ultimately bring my feelings in compliance with my earlier faith. The Deacons of the church requested that I return to the church, yet believing in their heart of hearts (by majority) that the decision to re-invite me to serve was beyond their scope of influence. The deacons decided it was the church's decision to reaffirm my call to pastor and not their decision to make. I was flown in and asked to stand before the church and share my conviction. I was met with compassion by some and vitriol by others. After a few minutes, I was excused to the pastor's study, where I waited, while the church deliberated on my fate. I thought to myself, "Now God, what are you going to do with this?" A few minutes later, the deacon chair met me in the pastor's study and said to me, "Brother Pastor, on a second vote, the church has once again called you to be the next pastor." While the call to serve was reaffirmed by the church, like the former church, this created trust issues, judgement issues, and character issues. Some members of the church raised questions about pastoral instability. I can go on. Imagine preaching to a fractured congregation. Imagine serving in ministry under the scrutiny of a hurting church. Yes, the church overwhelmingly reaffirmed the call, but the fallout from this action created space for pain and suffering. Loss of members, loss of what could have been.

To add to my distress, there was also pain and suffering in my family. The former church was the only church that my children knew. They experienced difficulty and pain as they struggled to establish connections in the new church. I experienced the loss of invitations to preach at revivals across the nation. News of my situation had spread. As a result, I experienced a sense of rejection by my Baptist convention on district and national levels. The dynamics were systemic; every human emotion emerged: good and bad, evil and holy, joy and pain. I wear this *past faith misstep* every Sunday when I stand and everywhere I am invited to preach.

Serving Grace and Loving God in the Season

There is a grace in all of this. God continues to use me in His service. In many ways, I'm ashamed to use *suffering in ministry* in the same sentence as *while serving*. I am learning during this long season that with God, *suffering and pain* are not dynamic equivalents. Suffering is meaningless, but pain, on the other hand, is redemptive. While it was a season of God's own choosing, as already stated, I take full responsibility for my mishandling the ministry of departure. My feelings collided with my faith. The "off-season" for me has become God's due season. My misstep was that I had difficulty in letting go. Yet God's faithfulness has never failed me! While I look forward to a Day of Reconciliation as God will have it, *all this is from God, who through Christ reconciled us to Himself and gave us the ministry of reconciliation* 2 Cor. 5:18 ESV.

If reconciliation is not to happen, I'm thankful nonetheless for God's faithfulness in allowing me to continue to serve while in the pain and the suffering that came along with my situation. Waking up to this reality was healthy for me because it allowed me to appreciate that much more the love God has for me, and the love I have experienced from both churches, including by the grace of God, the churches I was able to plant. After all, kingdom work has no address, only expansion "...*Thy kingdom come thy will be done in earth as it is in heaven Amen.* Matthew 6:10

Chapter 14

Rev. Frank White

Rev. Frank White

Rev. White is a native of Washington, North Carolina. He accepted Christ as his personal Lord and Savior early in his childhood and answered the call to the ministry in 1986 at the age of 19.

His academic achievements include obtaining a Bachelor of Arts Degree from the University of North Carolina in Greensboro, North Carolina; a Juris Doctorate Degree from North Carolina Central University School of Law in Durham, North Carolina; and a Master of Divinity Degree with Biblical Language from Southeastern Baptist Theological Seminary in Wake Forest, North Carolina.

Rev. White is involved in several civic groups and organizations in the local community. He is a member of Omega Psi Phi Fraternity, Incorporated, served as past president of the Raleigh Interdenominational Ministerial Alliance, and is currently an adjunct professor at Saint Augustine's University in Raleigh, N.C.

Rev. White is also the Pastor and founder of Antioch Bible Fellowship in Raleigh, North Carolina, a ministry that focuses on spiritual intentionality and the discipleship process. Through the teaching and preaching of God's Word, souls are being saved and lives are being impacted for the Kingdom.

Pastor White is born again, Spirit-filled, and appointed by God to preach the unadulterated word of God. He truly loves the Lord and feels that the best sermon preached is one living a lifestyle that exemplifies Christ. Rev. White is married to Margaret Ferguson White, and they are the parents of two children: Breiá and **Frank** Jr.

Triumphantly Traversing the Trauma

The pandemic that was brought on by COVID-19 was instrumental in helping me make sense of a number of things that were going on in my life. In many respects, it aided me in the understanding and processing of key events that had taken place. As a result, I was able to come to grips with the importance of learning how to navigate and negotiate life when dealing with the following-- (a) PERSONAL PROBLEMS; (b) PECULIAR PEOPLE; and (c) PROPHETIC PURPOSE.

On a personal level, the events surrounding the pandemic could not have happened at a worse time. I was still in the healing process and adjusting to the rigors associated with full-time pastoring. I remember attending a men's conference wherein one of the speakers advised everyone in the room not to be surprised when life suddenly takes an unexpected change. The speaker had been blindsided by a series of events that caused him to, in his own words, "pastor differently." The key in all of this, was expecting too much of the people he served. He went on to share that people will be people, but he discovered that despite that, God was still God. The speaker admonished all of us to expect the same or similar at some point in our ministries.

I learned firsthand what he was talking about during the pandemic—people can be peculiar. As a pastor, I have always ascribed to the belief that fulfilling The Great Commission should be the driving force behind ministry. To this point, when we planted Antioch in 2003, there was a great deal of attention placed on spiritual intentionality and the discipleship process. This entailed not only being a committed attendee while in worship but living a committed lifestyle that carried over in every aspect of a person's life. Accordingly, it was understood that spiritual disciplines such as daily prayer, personal Bible study, and occasional fasting were to be understood as vital for one's personal growth and development.

Although we were unable to meet in person for a season during COVID-19, I was confident that all would be well once we reopened. Needless to say, I was astounded by what I saw when we received the green light. To my surprise, even with COVID protocols in place, only about one-third of our pre-COVID crowd returned. Where were all of God's people? Surely, they were going to return. After a month, it became abundantly clear, many were not coming back. A good number of them had simply moved on. Some to other ministries, while others weren't attending anywhere at all. They were simply living their best life.

To be perfectly honest with you, I learned what it meant to be "all up in my feelings." I had heard this term used multiple times when people were describing how they responded to moments of disappointment and being let down. Now, it was my turn. "No not you!" One of my pastor friends exclaimed. "Nothing ever bothers you, **Frank**!" Well, this time was different. As much as I tried to, I couldn't help but think about the number of times that I had interrupted family time, or adjusted my schedule to make sure that they had appropriate pastoral support. All of this was magnified when viewed through the lens of what took place in my life for six months in 2017. This moment truly helped me understand my prophetic purpose.

As I reflect on it, 2017 started out with a bang. I was honored to be asked to share a Word at a joint Watchnight Service among several churches. I felt that the message the Lord had given me that night would encourage and inspire God's people. Using Psalm 121 as the text, I spoke from the subject, "Keep Your Head Up." Indeed, as I ministered that night, I felt a special anointing upon me as I reminded God's people that our help comes from the Lord.

I was led to share that sometimes we come face-to-face with the realities of the human condition which often present themselves when we are forced to deal with challenging circumstances. If left unchecked they threaten our understanding of both who and whose we are, and the peace that we enjoy as a result of our spiritual birthright. This will ultimately give rise to a scenario which involves the interplay of the following:

CHALLENGES- In this life, we are going to be periodically challenged. They are called trials. For this reason, James 1:3 tells us that "the trying of your faith worketh patience." Trials should not be seen as pitfalls or purely problematic as they typically are presented, but rather as an opportunity to grow and mature spiritually. Accordingly, we must learn to see these moments as a means of stretching our faith!

CHANGES- Again, it is important to note that God will use trials and tribulations to not only grow, but in some cases, groom us! It is to get you ready for that next level for which we might have been aspiring spiritually. Oftentimes, this process involves elevating our thinking from the perspective of the "old man" to that which represents the fruit of having a renewed mind.

CHOICES- When we are truly led by the Spirit, we will make the right choices. I was taught that a right choice will always be a rewarding choice! When challenged, instead of allowing people to take you through changes, we are to make the choices that will enable us to prosper by patterning ourselves after the example of Christ.

As I left the service that night, I was filled with a sense of excitement knowing that I would be celebrating my 50th birthday in a matter of weeks. To me, the sky was the limit, and I was looking for the Lord to do some awesome things in my life. Yet, within a matter of weeks, it seemed like life came to a screeching halt-- I got sick.

Prior to this, I noticed that after eating certain kinds of food, I didn't feel well. Because it didn't last long, I chose to ignore it. However, on the day in question, I knew something was terribly wrong. After eating a sausage biscuit, my heart was beating so fast that it felt like it was going to come out of my chest. I would discover almost six years later that it was due to a malfunctioning gallbladder, but at that moment I thought I was going to leave this earth.

As I sat there waiting to be seen by a doctor in the emergency room, the entire moment seemed so surreal. I had been there literally hundreds of times before as a pastor, but never as a patient. After a series of tests, I was told I would have to stay overnight. "Not me!!" I thought to myself, but then almost out of nowhere, I uttered the words, "This can't be happening… again."

This scenario was somehow reminiscent of what had played out over 30 years earlier in my hometown hospital ER. I was in my senior year of high school and being recruited to play football by several Division I schools. The injury being treated that night would ultimately spell the end of my football career. I distinctly remember being told by the attending physician, "Son, I would prepare to do something else, if I were you." His words, along with the direct and matter-of-fact means in which he shared them, left me feeling numb and questioning my future. How was I going to pay for college? Although I was a pretty good student, there were too many examples in my hometown of individuals who despite demonstrating great promise and potential, found themselves unable to leave after completing high school. In my mind, that scholarship was my ticket out of there. Thankfully, God had a plan for my life. I would eventually come to appreciate all that had taken place not only then, but also many times throughout my life. They all served to show His faithfulness.

After being released from the hospital the following day, I went through a season that was marked with additional ER visits, endless tests, and a treatment regimen that only made my condition worse. In fact, it was only when I made the decision to stop taking a certain medicine that my condition began to improve. By then, I had lost over 40 pounds and had begun to question if I would survive this ordeal. More than anything, it was having to endure what I now refer to as the "night season" that caused me to look at and approach life differently.

The night season changed my perspective on a lot of things. Throughout it, I spent a great amount of time reading the Book of Psalms. In fact, I was out of the pulpit and unable to preach for two months. A side effect of one of the medications was a wave pain that started within minutes of taking it. It literally felt like an elephant was standing on my chest. The discomfort lasted for approximately one hour and would be followed by a rapid heart rate of 120-130 beats per minute for nearly two hours. Because of the amount and frequency of medication, the cycle never really seemed to end.

From this experience, I came to appreciate Psalm 30:5(b) which reads- *weeping may endure for a night, but joy* **cometh** *in the morning.* I was unable to sleep and dealing with all of the things that I was experiencing at the time. I was not only tired physically, but also drained emotionally. More than anything, however, I was forced to face the fact that I could not turn off even when I wanted to. Consequently, most nights I found myself staring at the ceiling, able to hear my heart racing, and wondering when this would end. This would lead to endless tears which were followed by prayer. Although I would eventually drift off to sleep, it was not your typical restorative, REM sleep. Instead, it was nightmarish in nature, filled with doom, gloom, and destruction. I soon learned to value knowing how to pray and engage in spiritual warfare in the midst of my dreams. On occasion, I would awaken myself and tarry in prayer until dawn. Daybreak came to represent the fact that God watched over me and allowed me to endure to darkness and disconnect that accompanied the loneliness I felt during those times. And whereas I knew my family was close by, dealing with the totality of my circumstances— both the physical and psychological were only made bearable by knowing that God had indeed been faithful by allowing me to see another day.

In Psalm 119:71, the psalmist declares, *it is good for me that I have been afflicted; that I might learn thy statutes.* Prior to 2017, I had no idea the depth of the sentiment conveyed by these words. However, as a result of going through such a harrowing ordeal, I learned things about myself, and more importantly about the God of my salvation. Although I am certain that I had preached and taught from this passage many times over the course of my ministry, I had no idea that I would come to understand the true magnitude of these words. These exact words are echoed by the Apostle Paul in Romans 8:28 (NLT) - *And we know that God causes everything to work together for the good of those who love God and are called according to his purpose for them.*

All of this served to remind me and catapult me into my prophesied purpose. I say this because November 12, 2017, will forever stand as a bellwether moment in my life. For two months, I had been unable to do anything related to ministry. My breathing was shallow, and whenever I tried to do anything that required me to speak, I felt like I was suffocating. However, three weeks before, I started taking short walks in my driveway to build strength. Within three weeks, I was able to progress to a light jog. Where did all this energy suddenly come from? And why did I suddenly feel inspired to ready myself to return to the pulpit? Well God used a trusted friend who for more than 30 years has prayed for me daily. I will never forget the tone of voice on the other end of the phone, "**Frank** White. Hear the Word of the Lord! You shall live and not die! The Lord has healed you. Rise take up your bed and walk!"

Although we had prayed together many times before, there was something different about this one. After the prayer, the first thing I did was change my clothes. I wanted to embrace all that this Word meant for my life and ministry. I had to come to grips with the fact that God was not through with me yet, and I needed to get ready to proclaim the goodness of the Lord!

Over the years, I had been given words that served to remind me that no matter what, God had a plan and purpose for my life. When faced with the possibility of not being able to afford college, God provided me with the resources to not only finish college, but also earn a law degree and later complete my seminary training. At each juncture, I was blown away at the amount of resources He sent my way to ensure that I would accomplish every task that I had undertaken.

In this most recent episode, I thought about the people that God had strategically placed in my life to ensure that I made it to my doctor's appointments, provided me with proper nutrition, and even sat with me when all I could do was lie on the couch. God sent the right people to make sure I was alright. They witnessed firsthand the amount of pain and anxiety I had experienced, and their love and support played a major role in my recovery. Through them, I was reminded of how God knows what we need and when we need it, down to the minutest of details.

As I preached the message that day, I felt the presence of the Lord standing behind me. Although I was still finding my way through the process of recovery, I knew where my help had come from—it came from the Lord God Almighty who had made the heavens and the earth. Therefore, when the pandemic hit, I knew not to say, "Oh no, not again!" Rather, I knew it was yet another opportunity to stand still and see the salvation of the Lord!

Even now, I continue lifting, looking, and learning as I go. In many ways, the trials and travails of my season of sickness taught me how to traverse the trauma. I am a witness that God does indeed take care of His own—Hallelujah!

Chapter 15

Elder Bonita W. Womack

Elder Bonita W. Womack

Bonita Williams Womack is an ordained evangelist and church elder. Elder Womack resides in Willow Spring, North Carolina. She has ministered the gospel in foreign missions in Guayaquil, Ecuador. She is a noted teacher and trainer in the field of evangelism. Her desire is that she continuously and completely yields to the power of the Holy Spirit and that the ministry of reconciliation be manifested in her life and the lives of others.

She has studied management at the University of Notre Dame and is pursuing an associate degree in accounting from Liberty University in Lynchburg, Virginia. Elder Womack strives to live a holistic lifestyle and is an Independent Certified Optavia Coach.

She is the author of the book entitled, *Does Your Palate Need Cleansing?*

God's Grace is Sufficient

I received a call in February 2015 informing me that my mom had been admitted to the hospital. Her defibrillator had shocked her several times due to several cardiac events. I hastily prepared to take the over two-hour trip to Florence, South Carolina to visit my mom. On my way, I prayed to God about what was happening.

Upon my arrival at the hospital, I went straight to my mom's room. A few of my siblings were there with her. I had a very important conversation with my mom after my siblings left and I knew she was okay. I said, "Mom, I know you gave your life to Jesus a while ago, but do you know where you would have gone if your heart had not restarted today?" She responded, "You know, I thought about that today." I asked, "Mom if you don't know for sure, would you like to pray and make it right with God?" She said, "Yes!" I prayed with my mom as she recommitted her life to Jesus Christ.

Ephesians 2:8-9 (NIV) says- *For by grace you have been saved, through faith. And this is not from yourselves, it is the gift of God, not by works, so that no one can boast.* I am so grateful and thankful for God's unending grace.

It was a meaningful couple of days my mother and I spent together. I was thanking God for His grace and mercy as I drove back home to Willow Springs, North Carolina. He had given us more time. While driving home, I remembered a conversation I had with my cousin, Michelle. She reminded me that God had given us more time.

The Favor of God

My husband Bobby wanted my 50th birthday to be a memorable, grand milestone. It was just that! However, during the preparation for my birthday celebration, my mom was, once again, admitted to the hospital after many days of being in and out of doctors' offices for heart-related issues. Surprisingly, on the day of my birthday celebration, my mom showed up for my party, even in her weakened state. My mom pushing through everything to be there for me was priceless. My heart was overwhelmed with joy. Several friends and family members came to celebrate with me.

Also, I celebrated my birthday in the early part of June. However, for the climax of my birthday, my friends and I went on a trip, in the latter part of June. My mom had another week-long hospital stay, after my party, but was released before my trip.

I had a very disturbing dream in my hotel room during my birthday trip which shook me to the core! I dreamed several people I knew were hugging me, one at a time, and telling me how sorry they were. I listened more closely to what they were saying. I heard one after another, express, "Bonita, I am so sorry about your mom."

I was startled awake from my sleep upon hearing these sentiments expressed. My friends Sylvia, Trudy, and my sister-in-law, Toni were in the room with me. I told them about my dream. They consoled and prayed with me, encouraging me that things would be okay. However, God was showing me what would eventually happen.

The Last Dance

Each moment I spent with my mom was precious. I went back to Bishopville, South Carolina to my mom's home before embarking on my mission trip. Several family members were present, and we spent quality time with my mom doing what she loved. She enjoyed playing Spades and we played until 2:30 am, not knowing this would be her last time playing this card game.

I tried to spend as much time, with my mom, as I could before the Lord took her home. Once my vacation ended, I traveled to South Carolina every week to visit her. I made one final trip, on July 29th, with my niece Rachel to spend a couple of days with my mom. I was scheduled to leave on a mission trip to Guayaquil, Ecuador on July 25th.

The Midnight Knock at the Door

Our missionary team arrived at our hotel in Guayaquil on a Saturday evening around 10:00 pm. My roommate, Kimberly, and I were unpacking when we heard a knock at the door. I opened the door and to my surprise, my pastor, Apostle Phillip Walker, and our mission team lead pastors, Joe and Ronna Ferguson, were standing beside him.

I said, "We just got here. Has something happened already?" I knew whatever it was it was heavy because all three of them were at our door at midnight. I let them into the room and nervously asked what was wrong.

Apostle Walker asked me to sit down. He told me that my mom had passed and that they were there to pray with me. They all laid hands on me and interceded. This was exactly like my dream; they all began to hug me and tell me how sorry they were for the loss of my mom. All the air seemingly left the room when they exited.

When you lose a mom, there is something about that surreal moment that sucks your breath away. You must consciously remind yourself to breathe. I was struggling even though God showed me 30 days earlier that this would happen. It was still a shock and extremely painful. I was in another country to witness and tell others about the love of Jesus, and now the most important person in my life was gone. Christ was not gone out of my life, but my mom was. That night was filled with briny tears and excruciating silence.

Grace Under Fire

My pastor preached the following Sunday at a small, cinder block church named, Mucho Lote. No one expected me to attend service. After breakfast, I boarded the team bus. The church we visited was a recent church plant complete with plastic chairs and warm-hearted Ecuadorians. Our team regularly visited this church to support the pastor and congregation.

This was a delicate situation because that day, several former disgruntled members of that congregation who left the ministry were meeting us for morning worship. The worship before the sermon was powerful, led by their young adults. The atmosphere primed for God to move. The senior shepherd of this church, Pastor Ortiz, spoke in Spanish and our team interpreter translated.

It was an emotional service for me. Pastor Ortiz humbly asked his former members for forgiveness. He admitted that being a new pastor he had not always gotten it right.

He then shockingly gave the microphone to any of them that had anything to say. Many of them got up and filed to the front of the church. They all accepted his apology and asked him to forgive them as well. I have never seen the grace of God demonstrated so beautifully. The pastor, unfortunately, died six days later, the same day we buried my mom. I will never forget him or that service.

Suffering in Silence

There is something special about the first day of ministering on a mission trip. This trip was particularly different because I would be heading home soon to be with my family to bury my mom after only one day of mission activity. Ministering the gospel that day was so much easier for me knowing it was only for a day. I knew that my time was limited in Ecuador, so I had to make that single day count. I ministered to several people that day and several gave their life to Christ. Leading someone to the Lord is refreshing, especially at a time when you are in the middle of one of the darkest times in your life. I served all day while suffering through mixed emotions.

We went from one elementary school to the next, and I carried the love of Jesus every step of the way. The Spirit of the living God gave me hope and purpose like never before. God gave me strength to do as outlined in 2 Timothy 2:3(TLB)- *Take your share of suffering as a good soldier of Jesus Christ, just as I do.* I still had moments when I cried out because the grief was so hard to bear. I boarded the bus that evening with joy in my heart knowing that I had completed what God wanted me to do with the time I had there. God's grace is truly sufficient.

I was able to fly home from Ecuador the following day. It was a lengthy ordeal returning home by way of Bogota, Colombia due to hastily prepared travel plans. I was ready to go be with my family but sincerely missed the remainder of my mission work in Ecuador. I have a burning desire to see people set free and delivered. I was reminded of John 9:4 NLT- *We must quickly carry out the tasks assigned to us by the one who sent us. The night is coming, and then no one can work.* Time is truly of the essence even during our deepest hardship.

There were several people giving their condolences to my family when I arrived at my mom's house. Friends and family are a necessity during any crisis. I silently endured while simultaneously offering encouragement to my family.

The day of the funeral I felt as if I was walking through a fog. I knew that this would mark the beginning of the end. I struggled while preparing and planning for the funeral. I realized that I had been struggling since the knock at the door in Ecuador. I tried to be strong for my family who were also in distress. Oftentimes I feel there is too much pressure on the ministers in the families. People rely on ministers for strength, but sometimes ministers give out the strength we need for ourselves.

I remained silent, praying all the way during the journey to the homegoing service. I sought God for strength and courage to get out of the car. Entering the service was difficult. Sitting down in front of the casket made me both numb and overwhelmed. Nothing can prepare you for this moment. God showed me that it would happen, but He didn't tell me how I would handle it. He gives us dreams but not roadmaps.

After the service, I rushed to the family car because I did not have the strength to talk to the people when the service concluded. I almost screamed when a family member had to go back inside for the restroom. Immediately, people began to approach the car's open door. With tears in my eyes, I nodded and thanked them, but little did they know the magnitude of my *suffering in silence*. The entire funeral journey was extremely difficult. At times I was unable to vocalize words, while still trying to comfort other members of my family.

Returning Home

One of the first people that I encountered when I arrived at church, that Sunday, was Apostle Walker. He looked at me and said, "Now you know. You don't know, until you know, how it feels to lose a mom." That was such a profound statement to me, and the feeling is like nothing you ever want to experience.

The Grace of God

I would like to say that going through the loss of my mom was very difficult. Then I lost my nephew in a car accident only two months later. One of the hardest things I had to do was minister to my sister, Sadie, who had just lost her son. Tragedy had struck beyond our belief. On the same day, I spoke to my dear brother, Pastor John (Jay) Highsmith Jr, and he asked me "Did you speak to Dad?" Brother Highsmith's dad, Pastor John W. Highsmith Sr. was also my spiritual father. I said, "Not today." My "brother" asked me to call my spiritual father. He was resting when I called. I told Granny Muffin, the wife of Pastor Highsmith Sr., to let him rest, even though she offered to awaken him. I did not want to disturb his rest. This would have been my last opportunity to speak with him, as he transitioned the next day.

Pastor Jay was trying to tell me, but because I was already dealing with losing my nephew and still not over losing my mom, I could barely think straight. In hindsight, I could hear the urgency in his voice when he told me to make the call to his father.

On October 26th I lost my spiritual father to cancer. This took suffering to another level for me. He was ready to go home to be with the Lord although I had asked God to let him live. That week was one of the most difficult in my life.

I knew I needed to be with my family, so I traveled to South Carolina immediately. Every day I prayed for my spiritual father's family and was grieving with them as well. Both of the funeral services for my nephew and Pastor Highsmith, Sr. were on the same day in two different states. Somehow, I managed to drive back to North Carolina, on Friday, to be with the Highsmith family for the wake and drove back to South Carolina, late Friday night, for my nephew's funeral on Saturday. The only thing that kept me was God's mercy and His grace. I could have lost all interest in serving God but for His grace! In everything I experienced, I was never angry with God!

I believe with all my heart that ministering to others in distress is what empowered me. Listening to what God told me was paramount. You have no hope without a purpose. I was constantly reminded of my purpose. There is always someone going through something that can destroy them. I'm so thankful and grateful that after taking some time to grieve, I continued teaching, praying, and counseling others.

God kept me and I never stopped holding His hand during the process. There were times I asked God, "Can you use me after going through this?" I was encouraged by these words from Apostle Peter, *and after you have suffered a little while, the God of all grace, who has called you to his eternal glory in Christ, will himself restore, confirm, strengthen, and establish you.* 1 Peter 5:10 (ESV)

I give God strong Glory for allowing me time to heal from these great losses in my life. He pulled me away; he provided quiet times on many occasions allowing me time to be alone to grieve properly. Sometimes it's hard to grieve when you have so many responsibilities. I was a wife, a full-time employee, and an Evangelist.

Our titles do not eliminate our suffering when tragedy attacks. We are reminded that leaders are human too. At the end of the day, I was just Bonita. Suffering has a way of equalizing us all. It was God's grace that covered me during this time and continues to cover me. Psalms 34:18(NIV) *The Lord is near to the brokenhearted and saves the crushed in spirit.*

https://www.biblegateway.com/passage/?search=Ephesians%202%3A8-9&version=NIV
https://www.biblegateway.com/passage/?search=2+timothy+2%3A3&version=TLB
https://www.biblegateway.com/passage/?search=1pETER+5%3A10&version=ESV
https://www.biblegateway.com/passage/?search=PSALMS+34%3A+18&version=NIV

Chapter 16

Reverend Dr. James T. Worthy

Reverend Dr. James T. Worthy

James T. Worthy, a native of Charlotte, North Carolina, is currently in his 33rd year of preaching ministry and 12th year as the 11th Pastor of the historic St. James Missionary Baptist Church in Rocky Mount, NC.

Educated in the public schools of Charlotte-Mecklenburg County, Dr. Worthy holds several advanced and honorary degrees. He is completing the requirements to obtain his Doctor of Philosophy degree in Christian Organizational Leadership from Luther Rice College & Seminary in Lithonia, GA.

In September 1991, Worthy submitted himself to GOD's call to preach the gospel. He received his pulpit license from the Mt. Vernon Missionary Baptist Church of Charlotte, NC. The Lane Creek Missionary Baptist Association ordained him in October 1993.

An up-and-coming entrepreneur and businessman, Worthy is the owner and chief consultant for Third Eye Printing and Designs and A-scentuals Essentials and More. A published author, Worthy has two books to his credit: *When the Saints Go to Worship*, released in March 2010, and *Learning from Your Losses*, released in August 2021.

In addition to his pastoral and ministry labors, Worthy serves his community as a Faith Partner with the Down East Partnership for Children, a local facilitator for the All Pro Dads mentoring program, former Board Chair of PATCH, Inc. (Parents and their Children, Inc.), and former Chairman of the Steering Committee of Project GRACE, a local non-profit that addresses the health and socio-economic issues within the Twin Counties region of North Carolina. He presently serves as the Vice President of the Eastern North Carolina Ministerial Alliance, Statistician and member of the Executive and General Boards of the General Baptist State Convention of North Carolina, and on the Board of Directors of Ripple Effects Group.

With a heart and passion for educating, equipping, and empowering the next generation of preachers and pastors, Dr. Worthy is the founder and visionary of the Dear Young Preacher Mentoring Network and provides countless hours of support and guidance mentoring up-and-coming ministers to serve in excellence. Noted with many honors and accolades, he is also the host of the award-winning Dear Young Preacher Mentoring Talk Podcast, recognized as one of the "Top Ten" national mentoring podcasts in 2022.

He and his wife, Felicia, are the proud parents of two daughters and the grandparents of one.

Physician, Heal Thyself?

"All who were there, watching and listening, were surprised at how well he spoke. But they also said, "Isn't this Joseph's son, the one we've known since he was a youngster?"

He answered, "I suppose you're going to quote the proverb, 'Doctor, go heal yourself. Do here in your hometown what we heard you did in Capernaum.'" **Luke 4:22-23, The Message Bible**

As remarkable as it was that Jesus spoke with such wisdom at such a young age, how often is it overlooked in this passage the audience he spoke to and the message he rendered to them? The bold audacity of a young man to present a challenge to those who should have been challenging him. Recognizing them for their profession, he takes a moment to reveal a problem; they had been so busy healing in Capernaum that they did not see the necessity of caring for home. In essence, they could help others heal, but somewhere in the process, they did not take care of themselves.

WHO HELPS THE HEALER WHEN THE HEALER NEEDS HELP?

Looking back over my life and experience, this message that Jesus renders to the physicians can easily relate to my life, living, and lessons. And I must confess that the major lesson I have learned is coming to grips with the fact that while helping others become their HEALTHY SELF, I forgot to take a moment to remember to HEAL THYSELF!

Many times, our suffering while serving is self-inflicted. Our intentions are always to do the right things, but sadly, our choices and intentions are void of proper responsibility. In our pursuits to do and be great, we often place ourselves in positions where we contribute to our own pain. When I look back over my life, I can confess that I almost lost it all....my life, my family, my ministry, and even my character; trying to be all things to all people without being anything to enhance, empower, and educate me. What's worse was the season in my life, as a young preacher, that I became entangled with being all things to all people, engaged solely in trying to build a name/reputation for myself, engrossed in trying to make everybody happy, while getting caught up in the experience of hurting while helping...HELPING THEM HURT ME!

How did I allow myself to fall into the trap of *suffering while serving*? While it was easy to play the blame game, I immediately discovered that blame does not eradicate; it exemplifies!! In my attempts to please others, I was bleeding while leading. I was the one who was becoming weaker and weaker because my suffering was self-inflicted—battling low self-esteem, from the attacks of others, that resulted in the damaging effects of comparing myself to others and wondering why I could not be as successful as they were. I lost the comfort of being who God created me to be and allowed the antagonists of my life and ministry to affect my assignment through their destructive criticism. Thinking about a young lady who, very early in ministry, used these very words, *Physician, heal thyself*, to attack my ministry and preaching style. What's worse is that I allowed the words to become the knife that I used to puncture holes in my life, ministry, and character. I was dying emotionally, wearing a mask that all was well. Overcome with *should'ves, could'ves, and would'ves,* I became overwhelmed by the relentless attack of those who didn't know, care, or understand.

AND… just before I lost it all, I had a "Job moment!" I found myself asking God *why* he allowed others to attack me like this. And it was at that moment that God had to play "show and tell" with my life. God showed me that I brought my suffering on myself by telling me it is one thing to get caught up in what others say about you, what others think about you, and what others perceive of you… BUT!!!! That word helped me to control the bleeding and shift the suffering into supernatural release! God showed me that while I suffered, I was the one causing the damage, thus delaying my destiny. There was hope of me becoming my "healthy self," but first, I had to be willing to embrace the need to "heal thyself!"

Does my situation look/sound familiar? Are you reading this chapter thinking much like I did? Are you suffering from self-inflicted wounds? Is it you that is hurting you? Are you struggling to fill others but are empty from holes you have punctured into your container because you are taking the knife of others' negativity and bringing about the pains, perils, and punctures? THERE IS HOPE!! Healing is available. The helper can be healed to help others get healed. The reality and the hard lesson that I had to face, in the process to healing from my *suffering while serving*, was coming to understand that I could not heal without help! No matter how strong, smart, or spiritual we think we are, or even may be, we cannot heal without help!

Proper help produces prioritized health. It would be best to have someone who can see you at your worst and is willing to see you beyond your worst. Catch that concept… who's mentoring you? Who's holding you accountable? Do you have someone who has been where you want to go and is willing to hold you to a standard of accountability that allows you to heal yourself to become a healthy self? This was my first step in healing. A group of pastors and professionals held me to be better. Theirs was the threefold process of mentoring me from that dark space of blame and finger-pointing to a free space of accepting responsibility for my attitude, actions, and atmosphere. You can overcome when you have those who will celebrate, correct, challenge, and even convict you that your past is your lesson… NOT YOUR LIVING! They took on the challenge and assignment to help me see that just as quickly as I hurt myself, through facing the music and taking responsibility, I could experience healing!

How did I heal? I can tell you it was not easy, nor was it an overnight process. I still have some scars and reminders, but I am overcoming them by taking the same knives that I used to cause damage to carve out my destiny. The once-problematic blades have now prepared me to push, press, persevere, and progress to the point of power and promotion.

How was it done? What did I have to do? What powers did I have to possess (or, in some cases, repossess) to save myself from suffering while serving?

Reclaim your Power to say NO!

Healing begins when you embrace the revolutionary, revealing, and reviving power to say NO! So often, we bring self-inflicted suffering to ourselves because of our ability to attempt to be all things, be all places, take on all situations, and solve all the problems of others without leaving time for ourselves to revive, repair, restore, and renew. How often did I miss out on many events and special happenings because I thought, as the pastor/preacher, I "had to be there?" How many times did I push and press, even though I was physically weak and emotionally weary? How many times did I see the look of disappointment and rejection on the faces of my wife and daughters because I was everywhere for the people and nowhere for the "first ministry?" All the while, the same "Hosanna and Crucify Him" complex that Jesus encountered from the people he was sent to serve left me empty… suffering from the self-infliction of being a "yes" man for all the wrong reasons. Proper priorities taught me that healing begins when you use your power of saying no. Taking and making the time to rest, reflect, and rejuvenate is healing and therapeutic for you and those you serve. After all, just as you cannot fill others from an empty cup, you are just as ineffective if you are constantly pouring and never taking the time to be refilled and refueled.

Reclaim your Power to BALANCE

I grew up the son of a Baptist pastor. While my dad was one of the greatest to serve God's people, it came at a cost. I can vividly and fondly remember the evenings and nights that he could not spend the "quality" time we thought we deserved because he was studying, at the church in a meeting, or preparing for some moment in ministry. I remember Saturdays were spent away from the house without his presence because he was away in school, completing his undergrad and seminary studies. What's worse is that pattern continued in me as a father/preacher/pastor, to the point that I found myself repeating the pattern and continuing the curse of being an absent/unavailable father. I had good intentions, but my intentions were not always good for my family.

It wasn't until I had a "Come to Jesus" meeting with my wife that I realized that while I may have meant well, my actions were not well-meaning, and I needed to adjust. I immediately realized that it wasn't my practice that was off, it was my priorities. My desire to be all things to all people made me suffer, as a family man, because I was not providing the support that I needed to them. I had neglected the first ministry, thus creating an unnecessary rockiness that affected every area of my life. Reclaiming my balance had me in a place of taking a serious and close look at what mattered most. Too often, we go places for others, and in the process of making our name great, we lose out on what matters most. This self-inflicted suffering is common with young preachers. You mean well because you want to let the people know you are available, accessible, and even anointed, while those you serve are the antagonists to the first assignment. Don't allow those you commissioned to serve cause you to miss out on those you were called to serve. People will either embrace your priorities or reveal theirs in their refusal. You must make time for faith, family, fellowship, and fun. Physician, heal thyself!

Rely on the Power to TRUST GOD

The power to say no, create balance, and heal from self-inflicted suffering begins with knowing and understanding the source of your power. The strength to face your own music and, if necessary, change the station from shame and blame to promise and prosperity comes in being comfortable in everything you were created to be. How does that happen? You must rely on the power to trust God to make you everything HE created and commissioned you to be. Too often, we suffer in service because we build our name and brand by our standards, which are far too low compared to what God wants to do to and through you. It's easy to talk about what is wrong with others, but greater faith and trust produce the strength, courage, and wisdom to deal with what you know is wrong with you. I cannot count the times I heard God leading (telling) me to do one thing, but because I thought it would be a cramp in my style, I chose to do something different....and paid a painful price for it. A life free of self-inflicted suffering is a matter of trusting, leaning, and acknowledging (Proverbs 3:5-6).

Restore the Power of SELF-FORGIVENESS

Forgiveness is restoring or reinstating another to a rightful place or relationship after they have wronged you. Forgiveness is treating another as if they had never wronged you. We've heard and have been told we are supposed to forgive others. We have been told we are supposed to forgive and forget the evils others have perpetrated against us! But there is one sermon we do not hear much of; the need to forgive ourselves. In my life, the most challenging part of self-forgiveness came from falling into the false presumption that hanging on to the guilt of what I did to myself is helpful. By hanging on to the guilt, I somehow make what I've done wrong right... WRONG!!!!!

After so much covering my guilt with blame and shame, I found myself continuing to stab myself with the knife of self-injury, causing further damage and, in essence, falling deeper into suffering. SINCE GOD DOES NOT HOLD OUR SIN AGAINST US... THE TIME IS NOW THAT WE STOP HOLDING OUR SINS AND SHORTCOMINGS AGAINST OURSELVES! Since he has freed us, the time is now for us to free ourselves. The time is now that we begin to not only say it but act upon it… I FORGIVE ME!

There comes a time when we need to be able to forgive ourselves, learn from our mistakes, and then get on with life. Carrying guilt with you will not fix anything and will only hurt you. It will not change the past; it will only hurt you. It will not make the past right; it will only hurt you. The reality is GOD does not punish us based on what we've done nor deserve… if he did, all of us would deserve hell. Instead of God paying us back for the wrongs we have done, he loves us beyond our wrongdoing. When I think about what I deserved, compared to what GOD has given me… WHY AM I CARRYING WHAT GOD HAS ALREADY TAKEN AWAY FROM ME???? Why do we continue to linger and hold on to the very things that Jesus released us from through his death on the cross? It is almost like trying to clean a spot already removed.

At that moment, I caught a powerful revelation in self-forgiveness…all of us have our share of mistakes and failures. Instead of living in the guilt, we must be willing to shake it off, learn from the error, and keep moving forward. Don't allow anybody to hold it over your head or use it against you. Instead, grow from it, and it will enable us to make ourselves better.

A condemned person cannot enjoy freedom. A condemned person must face the consequences of his actions. A condemned person must live with the guilt of what they have done. But Paul reminds us, in Romans 8, that in Jesus Christ, there is NO CONDEM-NATION! If you carry the guilt of the past, today is the day to get rid of it. Remember, the process to a "healthy self" is found in being able to HEAL THYSELF! Despite the problems, the promise is still good. There is still hope for your healing if you are willing to put in the work. Be comfortable with who God created you to be. Take control of your life by repossessing the power over your life. Remember, you are not just a conqueror; you are MORE!

Physician, heal thyself? For a healthy self, it is worth the journey! Embrace and enjoy it. Your recovery will be a testimony worth sharing!

**A BOOK COMPILATION
FROM SPIRITUAL LEADERS**

SUFFERING *While* SERVING

**A BOOK COMPILATION
FROM SPIRITUAL LEADERS**

RESOURCES
For
LEADERS

Resources

This project has been presented to alert you that there is help for you. Many times, we lack assistance because of our lack of knowledge. We don't recognize the signs or behaviors that cause us to suffer, and once they are identified, we lack the information to help ourselves receive the treatment and action plans to heal. It is our hearts' desire that we all are made whole, not just through prayer, but treatment.

Here is a listing of national websites and phone contacts to get the help we all need. These agencies will be able to direct you to local services to begin the process of healing and deliverance. Remember, it's okay to love your Creator and still have an appointment with a professional to help you through your crisis. Please don't let another day pass without seeking someone to help you through your current situation.

RESOURCE DIRECTORY

National Alliance on Mental Illness- www.nami.org
- NAMI provides education, support, and advocacy for individuals and families affected by mental health conditions.
- Hotline Helpline: 1-800-950-NAMI (6264)

MentalHealth.gov:
- Website: https://www.mentalhealth.gov/
- MentalHealth.gov is a comprehensive online resource providing information on mental health, treatment, and available support.

Substance Abuse and Mental Health Services Administration (SAMHSA):
- Website: SAMHSA- https://www.samhsa.gov/
- SAMHSA offers resources, treatment locators, and a national helpline for mental health and substance use disorders.
- Helpline: 1-800-662-HELP (4357)

National Suicide Prevention Lifeline:
- Website: Suicide Prevention Lifeline- https://suicidepreventionlifeline.org/
- Helpline: 1-800-273-TALK (8255)
- The National Suicide Prevention Lifeline provides free and confidential support for people in distress, as well as prevention and crisis resources.

Crisis Text Line:
- Website: Crisis Text Line- https://www.crisistextline.org/
- Text "HELLO" to 741741
- The Crisis Text Line provides free, confidential support via text messaging for individuals in crisis.

National Institute of Mental Health (NIMH):
- Website: NIMH- https://www.nimh.nih.gov/
- NIMH is the leading federal agency for research on mental disorders, providing information on mental health research and resources.

Depression and Bipolar Support Alliance (DBSA):
- Website: DBSA- https://www.dbsalliance.org/
- DBSA offers peer support and resources for individuals living with depression and bipolar disorder.

Veterans Crisis Line:
- Website: Veterans Crisis Line- https://www.veteranscrisisline.net/
- Helpline: 1-800-273-8255 (Press 1)
- Text: 838255
- The Veterans Crisis Line provides confidential support for veterans and their families.

Psychology Today
- Website: www.psychologytoday.com

Recovery Centers of America:
- www.recoverycentersofamerica.com

Suicide and Crisis Lifeline: Dial 988

Remember, seeking help is a sign of *strength*, and these resources are available to provide support and assistance for individuals facing mental health challenges.

THANK YOU *For* YOUR SUPPORT

shero
publishing

Made in the USA
Columbia, SC
22 January 2024